La Dolce Diet

This book is dedicated to everyone who loves food but want to remain healthy by eating a balanced diet – here's to calorie counting that tastes good. Enjoy!

GINO D'ACAMPO

La Dolce Diet

100 RECIPES AND SIMPLE EXERCISES TO HELP YOU LOSE WEIGHT THE ITALIAN WAY

Introduction by Juliette Kellow BSc RD
Exercises by Nicki Waterman
Photography Peter Cassidy

KYLE BOOKS

First published in Great Britain in 2012 by
KYLE BOOKS LIMITED
23 Howland Street, London W1T 4AY
general.enquiries@kylebooks.com
www.kylebooks.com

10 9 8 7 6 5 4 3 2 1

ISBN 978-0-85783-098-2

Text © 2012 Gino D'Acampo
Book design © 2012 Kyle Books Limited
Photography © 2012 Peter Cassidy

Project editor: Emma Bastow
Photographer: Peter Cassidy
Designer: Jacqui Caulton
Food stylist: Gee Charman
Props stylist: Roisin Nield
Copy editor: Stephanie Evans
Production: Gemma John and Nic Jones

A Cataloguing In Publication record for this title is available from the British Library.

Colour reproduction by ALTA London
Printed and bound in China by C&C Offset Printing Co. Ltd

Acknowledgements

I know I am a little repetitive with my acknowledgements, but I am an extremely lucky man having the same special people in my life, and these books would be much harder to write without then. Their love and support means the world to me and it wouldn't be right not to continue to be thankful to them.

I need to start, as always, by saying a big thank you to all my family, especially my wife Jessie and my two beautiful boys, Luciano and Rocco, not only for tasting all my concoctions over the last few months but for also being everything I am and all that I live for.

Once again a big thank you to all the crew at Kyle Books who trusted me to write my sixth book, especially to Kyle Cathie, Emma Bastow and Peter Cassidy – wow number 6! To everybody in my food import company www.bontaitalia.co.uk who constantly support me in every way – grazie ragazzi! A special thank you to Abbi Rose-Crook, who helped me looked less glossy in a very hot Italy while doing the photo shoot – it's great having you around – and a massive kiss and a big thank you goes to my food stylist Gee Charman.

A huge bow to my fantastic friend and agent "The Don" Mr Jeremy Hicks – let's continue our success for many years to come!

And last but not least, I would like to thank all of you out there who, over the years, have continued to support me and enjoy my recipes. I had so much good feedback from my last diet book that I wanted to create another book for you to enjoy – here's to calorie counting again but please remain the women us men love!

www.ginodacampo.com
Twitter: @ginofantastico
Facebook.com/GinoDAcampo

Contents

What is La Dolce Diet?

After the success of my last diet book, *The Italian Diet*, I was told by many readers that they wanted more. People felt that it really worked – eating wholesome, delicious food but being much healthier with ingredients – and I was constantly asked when my next diet book was coming, so I took pen to paper, after many hours of spoon to pan, and have come up with a book I know you'll be pleased with. Rather than focus on typical diet ingredients, low fat ready meals and restrained eating, this book is a celebration of healthy food, the Italian way.

Creating a diet book takes more work that a 'normal' cookery book, especially if I've promised that flavours won't be compromised, so I did a lot of research to make sure I've got it right, both in calorie counting and taste. I have learnt so much on this journey. Certain ingredients featured in this book are so incredible good for you. For example, did you know that artichokes are one of the world's healthiest foods as they are high in fibre and antioxidants, are good for the liver, can aid cholesterol reduction and digestion, increase bile flow and help to prevent cancer – who knew? And guess what we now eat once a week! In this book I will not only look after your taste buds, while giving you 'diet' options and calorie-counted recipes, but I am also looking after your insides too!

In *La Dolce Diet*, which in English means 'The sweet way of dieting', you will find recipes that are full of flavour, easy and quick to prepare, yet light on calories. I have been testing these recipes on my family for months and no-one realised they were eating 'diet' meals, so I promise whether cooking for yourself, your family or for a party, no-one will taste the difference. Italians are one of the healthiest nations in the world and after delving further into ingredients used, I now know why and want to share my knowledge – I hope you enjoy it!

After six cookery books, I still remain focussed in using simple ingredients that require very little cooking, so my motto, as always, still stands ....

Minimum Effort, Maximum Satisfaction !

Enjoy and *Buon Appetito*!

Introduction

BY JULIETTE KELLOW BSc RD

This is a diet book like no other diet book. Right from the outset, *La Dolce Diet* promises that you won't have to give up on flavour or favourite foods to lose weight. Neither will you have to cook separate meals for yourself or eat dull, bland food while your family tuck into mouth-watering dishes. And we promise you won't have to spend hours trawling the shops for exotic and expensive ingredients.

Yes, with *La Dolce Diet*, you can wave goodbye to dieting misery and deprivation – and instead look forward to shaping up by eating like a true Italian. And by that we mean preparing and enjoying delicious dishes made from tasty, wholesome ingredients, that you – and your family – will love.

Most diets focus on telling us to 'give up' certain foods to shift those excess pounds – red meat, carbs, fat, alcohol, even entire food groups. Needless to say, we're usually faced with a 'banned' list of foods containing many of the things we love the most. You know the score – chocolate, wine, cheese, biscuits, bread and steak. It's no wonder then that with little pleasure left for cooking or eating we resort to calorie-counted ready meals, shakes and diet meals and snacks.

So welcome to *La Dolce Diet* where the emphasis is on eating more of certain foods – more vegetables, more fruit, more beans and lentils, and more seafood. More normal, everyday foods you can easily buy in your local supermarket! Better still, you won't have to give up all your favourites, survive on salad or suffer with meagre portions. Instead, you'll enjoy real food that tastes great and contains ingredients like olive oil, pasta, cheese and even, wait for it, double cream (yes, we know some low-carb diets allow double cream, but with *La Dolce Diet*, you're also allowed pasta and fruit to go with it!)

The reason for this approach is simple: ask an Italian to give up spaghetti, olive oil or Parmigiana and chances are you'll be met with a look of astonishment. You see, in a country full of pizza, pasta and red wine, Italians still manage to be one of the slimmest nations in Europe. Of course, not everyone in Italy is a perfect size but compared to other countries, there are far fewer men and women in Italy with a weight problem.

In fact, Italians don't diet – at least not to the same extent as men and women in many other parts of the world. And when they do need to lose a few kilos, they're less likely to turn to calorie-counted ready meals or diet products and instead continue to enjoy home-cooked food based on fresh ingredients and traditional recipes.

Italians certainly don't 'give up' anything in order to stay slim. Enjoying a delicious bowl of risotto, adding a sprinkling of Parmesan to pasta or drizzling olive oil over a salad is part of life. But – and here's the difference – Italians also eat a vibrant array of Mediterranean vegetables such as tomatoes, aubergines, peppers, courgettes and red onions. Lentils and beans are included in many dishes and seafood and fish play a much bigger part in the diet. Meanwhile, although olive oil is in every good Italian kitchen – and often used liberally in cooking – butter isn't usually on the menu. Portions tend to be smaller, too: pasta and risotto come in small bowls rather than on super-sized plates; and pizzas have thin, light crispy bases rather than stodgy, deep-pan ones, and come with just one or two toppings instead of every topping going.

So prepare to tuck in. It's simple! Eat like an Italian – and you can expect to look forward to an Italian figure! Now that's definitely *La Dolce Diet*!

Sizing it up

Italians are amongst the slimmest in the Western world. Fact! According to the World Health Organization, the figures collated for 2012 show just 17 per cent of Italians are obese. Within Europe, only France, Denmark, Holland and Sweden can boast slightly lower figures – and even then, when the numbers are broken down for men and women, it's only French women who are likely to have slightly trimmer waists than Italian ladies.

Across the rest of Europe, figures for obesity grow dramatically – 21 percent in Germany, 24 percent in Spain and 25 percent in the UK. Cross the water and it's a similar picture with 24 percent of Canadians, 25 percent of Australians and 27 percent of New Zealanders being obese. And in the USA, obesity affects a massive 32 percent of adults – almost twice as many as in Italy.

Unsurprisingly, the slimmer waistlines of Italians, brings them health benefits. To start with, Italian men can expect to live until they are 79, and women until they're 84 – that's an extra year compared to men and women in Greece, Germany and New Zealand, an extra two years compared with British women, and an extra three years compared to Americans. Far fewer Italians suffer with cancer, cardiovascular disease and type 2 diabetes, too – all conditions that are linked with being overweight.

Enjoy eating!

Extreme and faddy diets just don't work. Ask any nutritionist why depriving ourselves of our favourite foods leads to dieting disaster and you'll get the same answer. Quite simply, skipping all the foods we love quickly leaves us craving them so we end up bingeing. Then we feel guilty and despondent, so give up our diet, regaining all the weight we've lost, perhaps even with a few extra kilos.

The science backs this up, too. In one British study, for example, dieters had stronger cravings for the foods they were trying to avoid – and found it harder to resist these cravings – than women who weren't dieting. You don't have to deprive yourself for long, before cravings kick in, either. A Canadian study found women who 'gave up' chocolate for just one week consumed more once they could eat it again than those who weren't deprived. Similarly, adults who avoided all carbohydrates for three days and were then allowed to eat as much as they liked reported more carb cravings and ate significantly more once the restriction had ended than adults who kept on eating them. Bottom line: skip pasta for three days and chances are you'll end up eating a mountain of spaghetti.

The solution is to follow a way of eating that allows you to lose weight without giving up all your favourites. And that's exactly what *La Dolce Diet* does.

When it comes to shaping up, the only thing that really counts is calories. To lose weight, you need to create a calorie deficit so your body starts using up its fat stores to provide it with enough energy to function properly. The best way to create this deficit is to cut some of the calories from the food you eat AND burn more up by being more active.

Regardless of the diet you follow, this same principle applies, although most diets don't normally tell you this and instead come up with a faddy way to cut calories, often wrapping it up in pseudo-science. Think about it for a second and you'll see it's true: cut all carbs and you cut calories; survive on eggs and grapefruit and you cut calories; follow a detox and you cut calories; eat nothing but baby food and you cut calories. You get the picture – and it's a pretty gloomy one at that!

That's what makes *La Dolce Diet* so different from other diets. It works on the theory that as long as you slightly restrict your calorie intake – and do a little extra exercise to burn more calories up – you can lose weight without having to give up anything! Enjoying food with flavour is far more important to a true Italian than feeling deprived. That's why the recipes in *La Dolce Diet* still include ingredients such as olive oil, Parmesan and chocolate. And you'll find pages full of classic Italian dishes including pasta, risotto and pizza – not what you'd normally expect to see in a 'diet book'!

We've then built these recipes into a diet plan that restricts calories a little, allowing you to lose weight slowly but steadily at a rate of around 1lb a week – just like Italian mealtimes, we believe it's better to take your time and enjoy the experience rather than rush towards the finish line.

How have we done this? By controlling portions, using smaller quantities of high-fat, high-calorie ingredients (without completely cutting them out) and making sure meals are packed with flavour to keep your taste buds satisfied so that you don't feel deprived and tempted by fatty and sugary foods that come packed with calories but few nutrients. The result: delicious meals that will still help you to shape up.

The Italian Kitchen

It's perhaps no surprise that most Italian kitchens are filled with ingredients that form part of a traditional Mediterranean diet – a way of eating that experts around the world agree can benefit our health. Research back in the 1950s identified that people who lived in southern Mediterranean countries such as Greece and Italy were less likely to suffer with heart disease than people who lived in countries like Finland and the United States. One of the main lifestyle differences was linked back to a difference in the amount of saturated fats in the diet, with Italians and Greeks eating little and Finnish and Americans eating lots. Fast-forward to the present day, and 60 years of research has shown a Mediterranean way of eating has many other health benefits, too, including reducing the risk of high blood pressure, type 2 diabetes, certain cancers and even arthritis. Plus there's even evidence a Mediterranean diet might actually benefit waistlines – with Italians being good proof of this.

Sadly, eating habits throughout the Mediterranean, including Italy, are seeing a switch from a traditional diet to one that contains more convenience, processed and fast foods. However, Italians are certainly lagging behind this trend, with many remaining faithful to a traditional way of eating. According to a 2011 Mintel report, ready meals are still met with considerable resistance in Italy. In fact, Italians spent less than €5 per person on ready meals in 2011, compared with €17 in Spain, €26 in Germany, €34 euros in France and a massive €44 in the UK. Few homes own microwave ovens – instead, traditional family meals and cooking habits remain the norm and Italians are proud of their home cooked and local dishes!

So just what do you find in a traditional Italian kitchen? The answer is a combination of fresh, seasonal foods, a few staples that form the basis of quick, easy meals and natural flavour enhancers. Put all these ingredients together and the result is a balanced meal that meets international healthy eating guidelines, is packed with nutrients, and most importantly, tastes great.

The staples Pasta, bread, polenta and risotto rice are in even the most basic of kitchens. These foods are all low in fat and packed with starchy carbohydrates for energy – in fact, health experts recommend these foods form the basis of our meals. Better still, pasta has a low glycaemic index (GI). This means it releases its sugars into the blood slowly and steadily, helping you stay fuller for longer, so you're less likely to snack. Follow the Italian way of cooking pasta and keep it al dente (firm), too. Overcooked pasta has a higher GI because more of the starch is broken down into sugar and so causes bigger rises and drops in blood sugar. In other words, soggy spaghetti won't keep you as full as al dente spaghetti!

Pulses Most Italian kitchens have a supply of beans and lentils – dried and canned. As well as being low in fat, these foods provide a hunger-busting combo of protein and fibre, which helps to improve satiety, or that feeling of fullness after eating. Plus they're packed with a range of essential vitamins and minerals, including iron, which helps to keep blood healthy and prevents anaemia, bone-building magnesium and phosphorus, and copper, sometimes called the 'beauty mineral' because it's needed for healthy hair and skin.

Meat, poultry and fish Traditional Mediterranean diets tend to include small amounts of meat with more poultry and seafood – and this is still the case for many Italian kitchens according to the European Nutrition and Health Report, which found Italians eat less red meat than many other European countries, including France and most parts of Northern Europe. In contrast, Italians eat a lot more seafood, easily managing the recommended two portions of fish a week. Plus much of the fish eaten in the Mediterranean such as sardines, pilchards, anchovies, whitebait and fresh tuna, is rich in omega-3 fats, the type that's important for a healthy heart.

Eggs Italians tend to eat around 10 eggs a month, compared to just seven in the UK and this is actually good news for waistlines. Increasingly, research shows that people who eat eggs, especially for breakfast, tend to find it easier to manage their weight. In particular, it's thought the specific make-up of the protein in eggs is superior to the protein in other foods like chicken, for keeping hunger at bay, which in turn results in less snacking and so fewer calories. Plus eggs come in a ready-packaged portion making it easy to control the amount you eat.

Dairy products Although Italians tend to eat more cheese than many other European countries including France and the UK, overall they tend to have smaller amounts of other dairy products such as milk and yogurt in their diet. Together with less meat and low intakes of butter, this helps to explain why Italians have one of the lowest intakes of saturated fats in Europe – less than 11 percent of calories come from saturates in a typical Italian's diet. That's well within the guidelines recommended for good health, and considerably less than France, where more than 14 percent of calories come from this artery-clogging fat. Don't dismiss dairy products though – studies show that low-fat milk can help people to lose weight more effectively, especially from their tummies.

Fruit and veg Italian diets are packed with an abundance of vegetables – tomatoes, onions, courgettes, aubergines, peppers, celery, fennel, cavolo nero, spinach, broccoli and artichokes, for example – and fruits such as figs, apricots, oranges, peaches, plums, pears, apples, melon and pomegranates. This is great news if you need to lose weight because all these foods are low in fat and calories, but packed with fibre to help fill you up. But that's not all. Fruit and veg are also rich in a range of vitamins and antioxidants – nutrients that are proven to keep us healthy. Tomatoes – the foundation of many Italian dishes – for example, are rich in vitamin C and an antioxidant called lycopene, which has been shown to help reduce the risk of some cancers, especially prostate cancer, and protect the skin from sun damage. In fact, Italy is one of the few countries where more than 400g of fruit and veg are eaten each day – the amount recommended by the World Health Organization, which is translated in the UK into a recommendation of five portions of fruit and veg a day. That's way more than Brits who don't even manage 300g of fruit and veg daily.

Flavour enhancers Walk into any Italian kitchen and wonderful aromas are guaranteed to hit you. Olive oil, garlic, lemons, dried porcini mushrooms, balsamic vinegar, fresh herbs, olives, black pepper, Parmesan, capers – they're all in plentiful supply and add bags of flavour to meals. Better still, with the exception of olive oil and Parmesan, most Italian ingredients that add flavour to foods, add few calories.

Wine Italians tend to enjoy a glass of wine with meals (as well as adding it to their cooking to add flavour to pasta sauces, for example) rather than binge drinking. This means they don't consume anywhere near as much alcohol as many other countries. These facts are supported by figures from the World Health Organization, which reveal that Italians consume on average 19 units of alcohol a week – equivalent to around two bottles of red wine a week (with an alcohol content of 12 percent). In contrast, French adults consume an average of 24 units a week and Brits, more than 25 units a week. Red wine in particular is a good choice as it contains heart-healthy antioxidants.

Eat like an Italian

It's not just what Italians eat that affects their waistlines – it's also how they prepare their meals and then eat them. To start with, Italians are more concerned with quality than quantity. This means portion sizes tend to be smaller. They also like to keep meals simple, with few ingredients – pasta with tomato sauce, a bean stew, or grilled meat with salad, for example.

When it's time to eat, Italians savour their meals – they don't eat dinner in front of the TV or while on their computer. The whole family sit around the table together, including the children – Italian mammas certainly don't cook separate meals for their kids – and take their time, enjoying the whole experience. This is great news for waistlines as eating at a leisurely pace means we recognise when we are getting full and so stop eating earlier.

Breakfasts (*Colazione*) tend to be relatively small with coffee – either an espresso, caffé latte or cappuccino, without whipped cream or syrupy sauces! Cereal and muesli with milk and fruit are increasingly seen at the breakfast table, although cornettos (the Italian form of croissants) are a popular choice – but unlike other countries, they're eaten without butter or jam and instead dunked into coffee. Occasionally, Italians opt for ciabatta bread with cheese such as ricotta or Parmesan.

Meanwhile, lunch (*Pranzo*) is still often considered the most important meal of the day. While sandwich-style lunches such as paninis are becoming increasingly popular in cities, in many parts of the country people still sit down to enjoy two courses. The first course (*Primo*) is usually something like soup or a small plate of risotto or pasta with a tomato or vegetable sauce. The second course (*Secondo*) is typically a small piece of fish, meat or chicken with vegetables or salad, again on a separate plate.

Dinner (*Cena*) is similar to lunch, sometimes with the addition of antipasto consisting of cold meats, cheeses and vegetables at the beginning of the meal, and then finished off with dessert (*Dolce*) that more often than not consists of fruit and cheese. That's not to say sweet desserts aren't eaten, but puddings such as tiramisu, panna cotta and gelato tend to be reserved for special occasions.

It might appear all these courses mean Italians eat more but in fact, they simply spread their meal out over several platefuls and courses rather than having all their food on one plate – starchy carbs in the form of pasta for example on one plate, then meat, chicken or fish on a second plate and vegetables on a third. This approach is actually great if you're trying to lose weight as it allows time between courses to recognise whether you're getting full. And if you have a big appetite it can fool you into thinking you are actually eating lots of food because it's served on several different plates.

Finally, snacks tend to be less popular than in other Western countries, and consist of fruit, yogurt, nuts or bread with tomatoes, although ice cream, biscuits and cake are sometimes eaten. Meanwhile, there's usually no snacking in the evening after dinner.

Easy ways to make Italian meals even more slimline

- Always measure out olive oil with a tablespoon rather than pouring it liberally from the bottle.

- Watch your serving sizes of pasta and rice – a cooked portion should be around the size of a tennis ball.

- If you're making pizza, keep the base thin and crispy and opt for just one topping in addition to the tomato sauce and mozzarella.

- Make your own pasta sauces, rather than relying on shop-bought ones. That way you can control the amount of oil that goes into them and add extra vegetables to help fill you up.

- Serve grated rather than shaved Parmesan and use the finest grating plate – you'll use a lot less but it will look a lot more!

- Swap some of the meat in stews and soups for beans or lentils and extra veg – an easy way to fill you up and cut calories.

- Swap a first course (*Primo*) of pasta or risotto for a bowl of soup – research shows that starting a meal with soup results in fewer calories being eaten in the next course because it fills us up – a simple and tasty way to cut down on calories without feeling hungry or deprived.

- Try wholegrain pasta for a change – it's higher in fibre and so more filling. Italians mix pasta into the sauce before serving so copy this and you probably won't even notice the difference.

- Copy Italians' daytime drinking habits and limit soft drinks, avoiding them altogether if you can. Try sparkling water with a squeeze of lemon juice if you want some fizz.

The 1,500-Calorie Diet Plan

THIS MEAL PLAN IS PERFECT FOR WOMEN WHO WANT TO LOSE WEIGHT. WOMEN WISHING TO EAT A HEALTHY DIET WITHOUT LOSING WEIGHT SHOULD FOLLOW THE 2,000-CALORIE MEAL PLAN ON PAGES 16–17.

Breakfast	300 calories
Lunch	450 calories
Dinner	550 calories
Alcohol	100 calories
Milk	100 calories
Total	**1,500 calories**

MONDAY

BREAKFAST
1 serving of Papaya and Lime Fool with Vanilla Yogurt (page 32), 1 slice wholegrain toast with 1 teaspoon honey and 1 small glass orange juice.

LUNCH
1 serving of Avacado and Smoked Paprika Bruschetta (page 83) and 1 apple.

DINNER
1 serving of Rolled Chicken Breast stuffed with Spinach and Rosemary (page 154), 1 large jacket potato and 1tbsp reduced-fat crème fraiche and chives, and steamed broccoli and carrots.

TUESDAY

BREAKFAST
1 Morning Bar with Pistachio and Cranberries (page 60), 1 small banana, 1 kiwi fruit and 1 small glass of orange juice.

LUNCH
1 serving of Maple Syrup and Orange glazed Chicken (page 50) with salad and 2 slices wholegrain bread. Followed by 1 small pot fat-free creamy natural yogurt and 1 slice canteloupe melon.

DINNER
1 serving of Seafood Pasta with White Wine and Cherry Tomatoes (page 108) and 2 plums.

WEDNESDAY

BREAKFAST
1 serving of Simple Omlette with Parmesan and Chives (page 22) and 1 small glass orange juice.

LUNCH
1 serving of Beans, Tuna and Roasted Chicory Salad (page 55) and 1 pear.

DINNER
1 serving of Skewered Meatballs with Minted Yogurt (page 158) with 1 wholemeal pitta and salad. Followed by 1 bowl of strawberries with 1 scoop vanilla ice cream.

The 1,500-Calorie Diet Plan

BREAKFAST

1 serving of Kiwi, Mango and Strawberry Stir-Fry with Vanilla Yogurt (page 30) and 1 small glass tomato juice.

LUNCH

1 wholemeal pitta filled with 1 serving Carrot Salad with Mint and Honey (page 56). Followed by 1 small banana and 1 small pot fat-free creamy natural yogurt.

DINNER

1 serving of Baked Fillet of Cod in Spicy Red Salsa (page 152) with 8tbsp boiled rice and steamed green beans. Followed by 1 bowl of strawberries.

BREAKFAST

1 serving of Creamy Chocolate Rice Pot with Raspberries and Almonds (page 36) and 1 small banana.

LUNCH

1 serving of Chunky Winter Vegetable and Cannellini Bean Soup (page 122) with 1 thick slice wholegrain bread. Followed by 1 slice canteloupe melon and 1 bowl of raspberries.

DINNER

1 serving of Veal Shanks with Pancetta and White Wine (page 134) with steamed cauliflower and carrots. Followed by 2 plums.

BREAKFAST

1 serving of Ultimate Breakfast Tomatoes (page 20) with 1 slice wholegrain toast and 1 bowl of blueberries.

LUNCH

1 serving Baked Red Mullet with Thyme and White Wine (page 85) with salad and 1 orange.

DINNER

1 serving of Shell Pasta with Cauliflower Pancetta and Parmesan (page 126) with salad. Followed by 1 bowl blueberries topped with 1 small pot fat-free fruit yogurt.

BREAKFAST

1 serving of Toasted Muffins with Bacon and Poached Eggs (page 24) and 1 bowl of strawberries.

LUNCH

1 serving of Baked Lamb with Potatoes and Pecorino Cheese (page 138) with steamed broccoli and 1 bowl fruit salad.

DINNER

1 serving of Mushroom and Peas Risotto (page 128) with salad and 1 apple.

The 2,000-Calorie Diet Plan

THIS MEAL PLAN IS PERFECT FOR MEN
WHO WANT TO LOSE WEIGHT AND FOR
WOMEN TO MAINTAIN THEIR WEIGHT.
MEN NOT WISHING TO LOSE WEIGHT
SHOULD INCLUDE BIGGER SERVINGS OF
PASTA, RICE AND POTATOES.

Breakfast	400 calories
Lunch	550 calories
Dinner	750 calories
Alcohol	200 calories
Milk	100 calories
Total	**2,000 calories**

MONDAY

BREAKFAST
1 serving of Honey Pancakes with Banana Jam (page 33) with 1 bowl of blueberries and 1 small pot fat-free creamy natural yogurt.

LUNCH
1 serving of Pasta with Mozzarella, Cherry Tomatoes and Basil (page 40) with salad and 1 small banana.

DINNER
1 serving of Simple Chicken and Saffron Risotto (page 127) with a rocket salad. Followed by 3 Mini Chocolate and Nut Bites (page 180).

TUESDAY

BREAKFAST
1 serving of Dried Fruit Compote with Cinnamon and Yogurt (page 34) and 1 small glass of orange juice.

LUNCH
1 serving of Onion and Bacon Soup (page 124) with 2 thick slices wholegrain bread and 1 small banana.

DINNER
1 serving of Grilled Tuna Steak with Garlic Breadcrumbs (page 86) with 5 boiled new potatoes in their skins and salad. Followed by 1 chopped pear and 1 scoop vanilla ice cream.

WEDNESDAY

BREAKFAST
1 serving of Italian Style Omlette with Cherry Tomatoes and Parmesan (page 23) and 1 small glass orange juice.

LUNCH
1 serving of Lemon Couscous Salad with Artchokes and Cherry Tomatoes (page 42) and 1 slice canteloupe melon.

DINNER
1 serving of Pasta with Pancetta, Eggs and Mushrooms (page 105) with salad. Followed by 1 bowl fruit salad topped with 1 small pot fat-free creamy natural yogurt.

The 2,000-Calorie Diet Plan

THURSDAY

BREAKFAST
1 slice wholegrain toast with 1tsp butter and 1 boiled egg and 1 serving of Pears poached with Blackberries and Apple Juice (page 68).

LUNCH
1 serving of Stuffed Savoury Cake with Mozzarella and Semi-dried Tomatoes (page 44) with salad and 1 orange.

DINNER
1 serving of Hunter's-style chicken with Pancetta and Tomatoes (page 133) served with 6tbsp boiled rice and salad. Followed by 1 serving of Strawberry and Amaretto Eton Mess (page 181)

FRIDAY

BREAKFAST
1 serving of Toasted Country-Style Bread with Tomato and Basil (page 27).

LUNCH
1 serving of Roasted Aubergines and Red Onions with Goat's Cheese (page 46) and 2 plums.

DINNER
1 serving of Salmon and Leek Parcels with Smoked Paprika (page 114) with salad. Followed by 1 serving Chocolate and fresh Strawberry Cake (page 172).

SATURDAY

BREAKFAST
1 serving of Baked Eggs in White Truffle Oil (page 26) and 1 kiwi fruit.

LUNCH
1 serving of Sliced Steak with Rocket Leaves and Pesto Dressing (page 94). Followed by 1 bowl strawberries topped with 1 small pot fat-free creamy natural yogurt and 1tsp honey.

DINNER
1 serving of Thin-crust Pizza with Mozzarella, Cherry Tomatoes and Pesto (page 102) with salad. Followed by 1 bowl raspberries with 1 scoop vanilla ice cream.

SUNDAY

BREAKFAST
1 serving of Chocolate and Vanilla Pancakes (page 177).

LUNCH
1 serving of Slow cooked Squid in Spicy Tomato Sauce (page 140) with 6tbsp cooked rice and salad. Followed by 2 plums.

DINNER
1 serving of Artichoke and Butternut Squash Risotto (page 130) with salad and 1tbsp Parmesan shavings. Followed by 1 serving of Strawberries in Cointreau with Crunchy Topping (page 182).

Breakfast

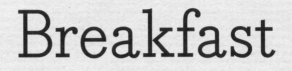

Pomodori ripieni con uova strapazzate

The ultimate breakfast tomatoes

Whenever I am away and have to order breakfast, I always opt for smoked salmon and scrambled eggs. Since I eat this a lot, I decided to create the absolutely ultimate way to serve it; you can't get posher than this. The combination of flavours is wonderful and the look of it is just a wow, so definitely serve this on a special occasion or for a special person. Remember, though, also look after yourself now and again too!

Serves 4

210 cals	12.3g fat	4.4g saturates	3.9g sugar	2.4g salt

4 large round tomatoes

4 large eggs

2 egg whites

150g sliced smoked salmon, cut into small strips

4 tablespoons skimmed milk

1 tablespoon butter

2 tablespoons finely chopped chives

Salt and freshly ground white pepper

1 Preheat the grill. Cut off the top of the tomatoes, about ½ cm from the top, and use a tablespoon to scoop out the flesh and seeds. Discard the tops of the tomatoes with the flesh and seeds. Place the tomatoes under the hot grill and grill for 4 minutes. Set aside and keep warm.

2 Meanwhile, put the whole eggs and the egg whites in a large bowl. Add the salmon and the milk and season with salt and pepper. Whisk together. Pour the egg mixture into a medium saucepan with the butter and start to cook over a low heat, stirring constantly with a wooden spoon. Continue to cook and stir until the eggs are set according to your preference. Please do not overcook the eggs, otherwise they will be dry and tasteless.

3 Fill the warm tomatoes with the scrambled egg and salmon mixture, sprinkle the chives over the top and serve immediately, accompanied with a small slice of toasted brown bread.

Frittatina classica
Simple omelette with parmesan and chives

A large egg contains only 93 calories and gives you over 6g of protein so an omelette is not only extremely easy to prepare, filling and tasty but very good for you. Like everything in life, you don't want too much of a good thing and too many eggs may be bad for your cholesterol, but you could enjoy this breakfast twice a week for a fabulous kick-start to your day, packed with much-needed protein. Use different cheese if you prefer.

Serves 1

| 239 cals | 19g fat | 6.4g saturates | 0.1g sugar | 1.1g salt |

2 fresh eggs

1 tablespoon finely chopped chives

1 tablespoon freshly grated Parmesan cheese

½ teaspoon salted butter

½ teaspoon extra virgin olive oil

Salt and black pepper

1 Break the eggs into a medium bowl and season with salt and pepper. Use a fork to gently whisk the eggs for 10 seconds. Add in the chives and Parmesan and whisk for another 10 seconds. Add the butter and oil to a 15cm diameter frying pan and place over a medium heat. Tilt the pan so that the base and the sides are well greased.

2 Turn the heat up to its highest setting and when the butter is foaming, pour in the eggs. Tilt the pan to spread the eggs evenly over the base. Leave it over the heat without moving and count to six. Tilt the pan to 45 degrees and use a tablespoon to draw the edges of the omelette to the centre. Tip the pan the other way and do the same thing. Tilt the pan again and flip one side of the omelette to the centre then fold again.

3 Take the pan over to a warm serving plate and the last fold will be when you tip the omelette onto the plate. Serve immediately and *Buon Appetito!*

Frittata all'Italiana

Italian-style omelette with cherry tomatoes and parmesan

On days when you aren't rushing off to work and want to pamper yourself, this is the breakfast to have. It is so filling and full of flavour and will definitely set you up for the rest of the day. You can be as creative as you like – try adding pancetta or roast vegetables or perhaps different cheeses. This is a meal for any time of day really, but it seems so much tastier first thing.

Serves 4

344 cals	21.4g fat	6.2g saturates	3.9g sugar	0.7g salt

2 large potatoes, Maris Piper or other floury potatoes

3 tablespoons olive oil

1 medium onion, peeled and finely sliced

5 large eggs

50g freshly grated Parmesan cheese

10 cherry tomatoes, halved

Salt and white pepper

1 Preheat the oven to 170°C/gas mark 3. Peel and finely slice the potatoes. Lay the slices in a single layer on a non-stick baking tray, drizzle with 1 tablespoon of olive oil, sprinkle over a little salt and bake for 15 minutes.

2 Meanwhile heat the remaining oil in a 20cm ovenproof frying pan with sides 4cm deep. Start to cook the onions over a medium heat for 5 minutes, stirring occasionally. Once ready, set aside.

3 Remove the potatoes from the oven and layer over the onions in the frying pan. Lightly beat the eggs with the Parmesan cheese, season with salt and pepper and pour over the potatoes and onions. Scatter the halved tomatoes on top, skin-side up.

4 Transfer the frying pan to the oven and continue to cook for 30 minutes or until the surface is lightly brown and set. Serve hot.

Uova in camicia
Toasted muffins with bacon and poached eggs

I couldn't compile a breakfast section without including a poached egg recipe. I don't often make eggs this way for myself but every time I do, I know why I should. The entire process takes less than 10 minutes and yet the result is a bit more special than the traditional fried egg and, more importantly, cooking eggs in water is so much better for you. Please use really fresh eggs – they are easier to poach.

Serves 4

| 278 cals | 13.4g fat | 3.9g saturates | 2.9g sugar | 2.9g salt |

2 large round tomatoes
8 bacon rashers, rinds removed
4 large eggs
2 breakfast muffins
4 teaspoons light mayonnaise
Salt and pepper to taste

1 Preheat the grill to medium. Cut the tomatoes into 8 thick slices and arrange on a small baking tray covered with a sheet of kitchen foil, along with the bacon. Set aside.

2 Place 4 poaching rings in a frying pan and pour in enough water to cover the base of the pan at least 1cm deep. Bring to the boil then lower the heat until the water starts to simmer. Gently break one egg into each ring and poach for 5 minutes until set.

3 Meanwhile, cook the tomatoes and bacon under the grill for 3 minutes on each side. Split and toast the muffins. Place a muffin half on 4 serving plates and spread the cut side with the mayonnaise. Arrange 2 tomato slices on top of the muffins and top with 2 rashers of bacon.

4 Carefully place the poached eggs on top of the bacon and sprinkle with a little salt and pepper. Serve immediately, with a glass of freshly squeezed orange juice.

Did you know?

To lose 1lb a week, you only need to drop 500 calories a day – that's the equivalent of a coffee-shop muffin! It might not sound much, but it adds up to almost four stone in a year!

Uova in coppetta con tartufo bianco
Baked eggs with white truffle oil

Whenever I make this for myself, I almost feel that I should be serving it with a glass of champagne. Whether that's because of the strong, elegant flavour of the truffle oil or simply because the dish looks so good I'm not sure, although I'm certain you will enjoy this and feel a little indulged afterwards. If you've never had baked eggs for breakfast, I hope it will be love at first bite!

Serves 4

370	cals	28g	fat	9.4g	saturates	1.3g	sugar	0.9g	salt

Butter, softened, for greasing

4 large, very fresh free-range eggs

4 tablespoons double cream

4 tablespoons white truffle oil

3 clices wholegrain bread

Salt and freshly ground black pepper

1 Preheat the oven to 190°C/gas mark 5. Fill the kettle and put it on to boil. Using a pastry brush, grease the base and sides of 4 × 130ml ramekins with the softened butter. Place the ramekins in an ovenproof dish with sides at least 8cm high.

2 Crack an egg into each ramekin, then add 2 pinches of salt, 1 tablespoon of cream and 1 tablespoon of truffle oil to each one.

3 Pour enough boiling water into the ovenproof dish to reach about halfway up the sides of the ramekins. Transfer the dish to the middle of the oven and bake for 14 minutes.

4 Toast the bread and cut each slice into 4 soldiers. Grind over a little black pepper and serve immediately with 3 toasted bread soldiers for each portion.

Tip

Want to wake up in a hurry? After your shower, crank up the volume on your favourite radio station, grab a towelling-robe, and rev up your body with some early-morning dancing to at least three songs – you'll burn at least 50 calories in 10 minutes too!

Bruschette al pomodoro
Toasted country-style bread with tomato and basil

It's funny choosing this recipe for my breakfast section as I always prepare this as a starter, but that's actually how the dish came about. I had some leftover tomato marinade from a party the night before, and woke up slightly worse for wear – and very hungry. I couldn't be bothered to cook anything, but fancied something really tasty so I grilled some bread and covered it with the tomato and basil – it was the best instant breakfast ever!

Serves 4

309	cals	8.2g	fat	1.5g	saturates	6.8g	sugar	1.5g	salt

500g small plum tomatoes

10 basil leaves, shredded

2 tablespoons extra virgin olive oil

1 country-style loaf of bread

2 garlic cloves

Salt and freshly ground black pepper

1 Quarter the tomatoes and place in a large mixing bowl. Add in three-quarters of the basil, the extra virgin olive oil and season with salt and pepper. Mix everything together and cover the bowl with a tea towel. Leave to marinate at room temperature for 10 minutes, stirring after 5 minutes.

2 Preheat a griddle pan. Cut 8 slices from the loaf, each about 2cm thick. Toast each side on the griddle pan until dark brown and crispy all over. Leave to cool slightly.

3 Lightly rub the garlic over both sides of the toasted bread. Place 2–3 tablespoons of the tomato mixture on each slice of bread and arrange the bruschette on a large serving plate.

4 Drizzle over any remaining juices from the bowl of tomatoes and sprinkle the remaining basil on top. Serve with a large glass of apple juice.

Scombro grigliato con semi di finocchietto

Grilled mackerel with fennel seeds and balsamic vinegar

When you fancy a savoury start to the morning, please try this. I love it: not only is it delicious but you can't get anything healthier. Mackerel is an oily, coldwater fish known especially for its nutritional benefits, as it's a great source of omega-3 fatty acids which are good for brain growth and protection. In fact, the omega-3 content may actually reduce your risk of developing Alzheimer's disease. If you prefer, you can make this with sardines (another oily fish) and sometimes I add capers for an extra kick.

Serves 4

425	cals	32.9g	fat	6.3g	saturates	1.2g	sugar	2.5g	salt

1 tablespoon extra virgin olive oil

2 tablespoons freshly squeezed lemon juice

1 teaspoon fennel seeds, crushed

Pinch of dried chilli flakes

4 x 350g fresh mackerel, filleted (giving 8 pieces in total)

50g rocket leaves

20g flat-leaf parsley

150g pitted Kalamata olives, drained and halved

1 tablespoon balsamic vinegar

Salt and freshly ground white pepper

1 Pour the oil into a medium bowl with the lemon juice, fennel seeds and chilli flakes. Season with ½ teaspoon of salt and a little white pepper. Mix together. Brush some of the marinade on both sides of the mackerel fillets and leave to marinate on a plate for 10 minutes. Preheat a griddle pan. Meanwhile, mix the rocket leaves with the parsley and arrange in the centre of 4 plates.

2 Place the mackerel fillets on the hot griddle pan, skin-side down, and cook for 30 seconds. Turn the fillets and cook the other side for a further 30 seconds. Transfer the fillets to a plate and break in half. Arrange the mackerel and olives on top and around the rocket and parsley salad, trying not to flatten the leaves too much.

3 Pour the remaining marinade with the balsamic vinegar into a medium frying pan. Mix and cook over a high heat for 30 seconds.

4 Spoon the hot dressing over the fish and leaves and serve immediately.

Frutta saltata in padella
Kiwi, mango and strawberry stir-fry with vanilla yogurt

I must admit that I originally created this recipe as a dessert and it was always a huge success, but lately I have been trying to be sure I have breakfast (typical Italian – a quick coffee and I'm off). On the mornings I make myself something like this tasty little dish, I definitely feel so much better. I'm not sure if that's because of the fruit it contains or merely that it gets your metabolism working but I promise you'll feel great after. Enjoy!

Serves 2

| 274 cals | 9.8g fat | 5.9g saturates | 40g sugar | 0.3g salt |

200ml low-fat plain yogurt

1 teaspoon vanilla extract

20g salted butter

2 kiwis, peeled and sliced into ½cm discs

1 ripe mango, peeled and sliced into ½cm strips

150g strawberries, hulled and halved

1 tablespoon caster sugar

1 Pour the yogurt into a small bowl and stir in the vanilla extract. Set aside.

2 Melt the butter in a large frying pan over a high heat and fry the kiwi, mango and strawberries for 1 minute. Shake the pan halfway through cooking. Sprinkle over the sugar and continue to fry for a further minute.

3 Divide the caramelised fruits between 4 serving bowls. Spoon over the vanilla yogurt and serve immediately.

Tortine dolci
Honey pancakes with banana jam

Pancakes should absolutely not be just for Pancake Day. They are so quick to make and you can be as creative as you like, pretty much anything goes, sweet or savoury. This one is a way of being a little more adventurous with everyday ingredients. I created this recipe as I love bananas. If you're out of honey use maple syrup, but go easy as it's much sweeter.

Serves 4

306	cals	6.1g	fat	3g	saturates	37.1g	sugar	0.5g	salt

for the pancakes

110g self-raising flour
Small pinch of salt
1 medium egg
1 tablespoon runny honey
160ml semi-skimmed milk
½ tablespoon butter

for the banana jam

200ml apple juice
1 tablespoon soft brown sugar
1 tablespoon freshly squeezed
 lemon juice
½ teaspoon ground cinnamon
4 ripe bananas
½ tablespoon butter, melted

1 To make the pancakes, sift the flour and salt into a large bowl. Break in the egg and pour in the honey and milk. Mix everything together to create a smooth batter. Leave to rest for 15 minutes. Meanwhile, put the apple juice, the sugar, lemon juice and cinnamon in a medium saucepan. Bring to the boil then reduce by half. Transfer the juice to a large bowl.

2 Roughly chop the bananas and add to the bowl with the reduced juice. Pour in the melted butter and mash to a smooth purée. Place a heavy-based frying pan over a medium heat and rub the surface with a little of the butter.

3 Using a small ladle, pour a few small mounds of batter into the hot pan, spacing them well apart. Once bubbles appear on the surface, flip the pancakes over and cook until set and golden all over. Keep the batches warm in a very low oven while you cook the rest.

4 Serve my honey pancakes with the banana jam and your favourite cup of tea.

Frullato di papaya
Papaya and lime fool with vanilla yogurt

Yogurt first thing in the morning is delicious but served up as a fruit fool makes it pretty special. I just love the tangy flavours of this combination – as I'm sure you will too.

Serves 4

160	cals	1.1g	fat	0.6g	saturates	16.8g	sugar	0.2g	salt

1kg red papayas
1 tablespoon lime juice
2 tablespoon icing sugar
1 teaspoon vanilla extract
350ml low-fat yogurt

1 Peel the papayas, remove the seeds and place in a medium bowl. Using a fork, mash the flesh until smooth. (Do not be tempted to use a food processor otherwise the fruit will be too runny.)

2 Pour in the lime juice and sugar and gently mix everything together. Fold in the yogurt and the vanilla and spoon the mixture into 4 dessert glasses.

3 Cover with clingfilm and place in the fridge until ready to serve.

Frutta pazza
Dried fruit compote with cinnamon and yogurt

If you find it hard to have your 'five a day', this recipe makes life tastier and easier. How about having all five for breakfast? This recipe is *fantastico* and the crunchy oats on top add great texture.

Serves 4

348	cals	4g	fat	0.8g	saturates	58.7g	sugar	0.3g	salt

130g dried prunes
130g dried apricots
130g dried peaches
50g dried apples
30g dried cranberries
500ml apple juice
1 teaspoon ground cinnamon
300ml low-fat natural yogurt
120g crunchy oat cereal

1 Place all the dried fruits in a large saucepan and pour in the apple juice. Add the cinnamon, place the pan over the heat and bring to the boil. Lower the heat and simmer for 10 minutes until all the fruit is tender.

2 Allow the fruit mixture to cool in the saucepan then transfer to a large bowl and refrigerate for 1 hour. (You can also prepare the compote the night before.)

3 Spoon half the compote into 4 dessert glasses then cover with half the yogurt. Spoon over the remaining compote and finish with a final layer of yogurt to cover the fruit. Scatter the oat cereal on top and serve.

Risotto al cioccolato
Creamy chocolate rice pot with raspberries and almonds

This recipe is dedicated to my son Rocco. On holiday he surprised me by going to get a huge bowl of rice pudding for breakfast. I was chuffed to bits as normally he's a chocoholic, but he soon ruined the illusion by pulling out six pots of chocolate spread, which he proceeded to stir into the rice. After that, he tucked in, finishing the lot. I was allowed a taste and had to admit that it was very good. Of course, I have made this recipe a little more elegant and have served it for breakfast and as a dessert.

Serves 2

216	cals	7.5g	fat	1g	saturates	15.7g	sugar	0.2g	salt

550ml skimmed milk

2 teaspoons cocoa powder

30g caster sugar

65g arborio risotto rice

3 tablespoons skinned almonds, finely chopped

½ teaspoon vanilla extract

60g fresh raspberries

1 Tip the milk, cocoa powder and sugar into a medium saucepan and stir over low heat until the sugar has dissolved. Add the rice and stir briefly with a wooden spoon. Bring to the boil and immediately turn down the heat to as low as possible. Cook for 30–35 minutes, stirring occasionally.

2 Meanwhile, place the almonds in a small frying pan and dry toast for 2 minutes on a medium heat, shaking the pan occasionally. Set aside.

3 Once the rice mixture looks all thick and creamy and the rice grains are tender, stir in the vanilla extract and raspberries. Remove from the heat and set aside to rest for 1 minute.

4 Spoon the rice mixture into two cappuccino cups and scatter over the toasted almonds. Serve immediately.

Tip

If you'd planned an early-morning workout, but you got out of bed in the morning in a bad mood or completely lethargic, get back into bed and try getting up again. Lie down again for a moment to shift your perception. Then translate that into movement and get up in a different way – either on the other side of the bed or from the bottom edge of the bed.

Lunch on
the go

Penne alla caprese
Pasta with mozzarella, cherry tomatoes and basil

This is such a perfect lunch to have on the go; the original pasta salad that will never bore you. The colours are so inviting and it's a combination that will fill you up without leaving you feeling heavy. You can use fusilli or farfalle pasta if you prefer but please remember not to over-cook it: soggy pasta cold is even worse than hot. This salad is also great with barbecued food.

Serves 4

468	cals	16.5g	fat	5.7g	saturates	5.1g	sugar	0.5g	salt

3 tablespoons extra virgin olive oil

1 garlic clove, peeled and finely sliced

300g cherry tomatoes, halved

350g penne rigate

10 basil leaves, roughly shredded

1 x 125g mozzarella balls, drained and cut into 1cm cubes

Salt and freshly ground black pepper

1 Heat the oil in a large frying pan and gently fry the garlic and cherry tomatoes for 1 minute, stirring with a wooden spoon. Season with salt and pepper, remove from the heat and set aside while you cook the pasta.

2 Bring a large saucepan of salted water to the boil and cook the pasta until al dente. Drain and tip the pasta back into the same pan.

3 Tip in the cherry tomatoes along with the basil and the mozzarella. Season with salt and a little more pepper. Remove from the heat and toss everything together for 15 seconds to ensure all the flavours combine.

4 Serve immediately or, allow to cool to room temperature then store in a sealed container in the fridge for the following day. Do not keep longer than 48 hours and always eat it at room temperature.

Tip

While waiting for the kettle to boil, squeeze your bottom really hard for 10 seconds. Do this five times a day and you'll notice a difference in tone in two weeks. This is because the muscles in the bottom will hold in a semi-flexed position for up to 20 minutes after working the muscle.

Insalata di couscous
Lemon couscous salad with artichokes and cherry tomatoes

So many people tend to overlook couscous, yet it's such a fabulous alternative to boring rice and is a great accompaniment to almost anything. I often make couscous salad with roasted vegetables but I wanted to create something fresher in flavour and I know you won't be disappointed with what I've come up with. You can make this dish all year round but it definitely makes you feel summer is here.

Serves 4

| 524 | cals | 29.8g | fat | 3.5g | saturates | 3.2g | sugar | 1g | salt |

250g couscous

325ml boiling hot vegetable stock

60ml extra virgin olive oil

Grated zest and juice of 3 unwaxed lemons

3 tablespoons capers in vinegar, drained

6 tablespoons finely shredded fresh mint leaves

50g pine nuts

6 artichokes hearts in oil, drained and quartered

20 cherry tomatoes, halved

1 Tip the couscous into a large bowl and pour over the hot stock. Cover the bowl tightly with clingfilm and allow it to rest for 5 minutes. Use a fork to fluff up the couscous and separate the grains.

2 Heat half of the oil in a frying pan over a medium heat. Add the lemon zest, capers, mint and pine nuts. Cook for 5 minutes then remove from the heat and allow to cool to room temperature.

3 Add the contents of the frying pan to the couscous with the rest of the oil, lemon juice, artichokes and cherry tomatoes. Gently toss everything together and serve.

Piegata con pesto rosso
Folded bread with red pesto and parmesan

As you may know from my last book, *Italian Home Baking*, making bread is a must in my house. The smell and satisfaction is just second to none. This recipe is a little time-consuming because you have to allow the dough to rise but it's still so easy and definitely worth it. I suggest eating it with some roasted vegetables for your lunch on the go but it's also amazing with any kind of soup and very impressive to serve warm for dipping into Italian extra virgin olive oil before a main meal.

Makes 4

| 596 cals | 15.3g fat | 2.3g saturates | 4.9g sugar | 2.1g salt |

500g strong plain white flour, plus extra for dusting

1 teaspoon salt

1 teaspoon caster sugar

7g (one sachet) fast-action dried yeast

2 tablespoons extra virgin olive oil, plus extra for greasing

300ml warm water

for the filling

60g red pesto

60g semi-dried cherry tomatoes in oil, drained

2 teaspoons freshly grated Parmesan cheese

Freshly ground black pepper

1 Brush a large baking tray with a little oil. Sift the flour into a large bowl, add the salt, sugar and yeast, and mix all the ingredients together. Make a well in the centre, pour in the olive oil and water, and with the help of a wooden spoon start mixing until all the ingredients are blended together, then transfer the mixture onto a floured surface and knead by hand for about 10 minutes until the dough is smooth and elastic.

2 Shape the dough into a ball and put back into the bowl. Brush the top with a little oil, cover with clingfilm and leave it to rise in a warm place away from draughts for 1 hour.

3 Turn out the dough onto a lightly floured surface and divide into 4 equal pieces. Cover with clingfilm and leave to rest for 30 minutes. Transfer the dough pieces to the oiled baking tray and, using your fingertips, gently press down each dough piece to create a disc about 2cm thick.

4 Spread the red pesto over the discs and scatter the semi-dried cherry tomatoes on top. Sprinkle over the Parmesan and a grinding of black pepper. Fold the discs to create 4 half-moon shapes, but do not seal the edges. Cover the folded bread with clingfilm and leave to rest in a warm place for 35 minutes. Preheat the oven to 180°C/gas mark 4.

5 Remove the clingfilm and bake the bread in the middle of the oven for 18 minutes. Allow to slightly cool on a wire rack and serve warm, or take it to the office the next day with a few grilled vegetables of your choice.

Torta salata
Stuffed savoury cake with mozzarella and semi-dried tomatoes

Spinach, tomato and mozzarella are a great trio and make a tart filling that's just to die for. You can enjoy it warm as an evening meal and then again the next day for lunch on the go.

Serves 6

481 cals	18.8g fat	7.2g saturates	2.9g sugar	1.3g salt

450g strong plain white flour

10g fast-action dried yeast

3 tablespoons extra virgin olive oil plus extra for brushing

300ml warm water

300g frozen spinach, defrosted

100g rocket leaves, roughly chopped

2 x 125g mozzarella balls, cubed

120g semi-dried tomatoes in oil, drained and halved

10 basil leaves

Salt and freshly ground black pepper

1 Brush the base and sides of a 25cm loose-based cake tin with oil. Sift the flour into a large bowl, and stir in the yeast. Make a well in the centre, pour in the olive oil and water, and with the help of a wooden spoon start mixing until all the ingredients are blended together, then transfer the mixture onto a floured surface and knead by hand for about 10 minutes until the dough is smooth and elastic.

2 Shape the dough into a ball and put back into the bowl. Brush the top with a little oil, cover with clingfilm and leave it to rise in a warm place away from draughts for 1½ hours until nearly doubled in size. Preheat the oven to 220°C/gas mark 7.

3 Squeeze the spinach to remove any excess water and place in a large bowl with the rocket leaves. Add the Mozzarella, the semi-dried tomatoes and the basil leaves. Season with salt and pepper and gently mix everything together.

4 Turn out the dough onto a lightly floured surface and punch down. Knead for 3 minutes then divide into two pieces, one slightly bigger than the other. Roll out the bigger piece to form a disc about 3cm larger than the base of the tin. Place on the base of the tin and try to mould the dough so that it lines the sides up to the rim. Spread the spinach mixture over the base, leaving a 1cm gap from the edges.

5 Roll out the smaller piece of dough to the same size as the tin, brush the edges with a little water and place over the filling. Press the edges together really well to ensure a good seal. Gently press your fingertips into the dough to make indentations then brush with olive oil. Sprinkle with the sea salt and bake in the middle of the oven for 30 minutes until risen and firm.

6 Remove from the oven and leave the torta to rest for 10 minutes in the tin on a wire rack to allow the air to circulate around it.

Melanzane e cipolle arrosto
Roasted aubergines and red onions with goat's cheese

When my wife was expecting our second son, she craved goat's cheese and of course wasn't allowed to eat any. So once Rocco was born, everything had to have goat's cheese on it for about four months (weird!). Anyway, as I absolutely love aubergines I wanted to create something we would both enjoy – and this is it. The flavours are incredible together. This dish is really versatile – try it as a great starter, accompaniment or salad – and I know it will become a regular recipe in your house.

Serves 4

512 cals	32.6g fat	9.7g saturates	10.3g sugar	1.6g salt

2 large aubergines

4 large garlic cloves, unpeeled

2 red onions, peeled and cut into 4 wedges

5 fresh thyme sprigs

5 tablespoons extra virgin olive oil

150g goat's cheese

40g pine nuts, lightly toasted

4 tablespoons flat-leaf parsley, roughly chopped, to garnish

8 thin slices of country-style bread, to serve

Salt and freshly ground black pepper

1 Preheat the oven to 190°C/gas mark 5. Prepare the aubergine by trimming away the last 1cm from both ends along with any green bits. Cut the flesh into 1cm round slices. Using the flat of a large chopping knife, squash the unpeeled garlic cloves to release their flavour.

2 Place the aubergines and the onions in a large roasting tray in a single layer. Scatter over the garlic and thyme. Drizzle over the oil, ensuring that all the aubergines are coated, and season with salt and pepper. Transfer the tray to the middle of the oven and roast for 30 minutes until the aubergines are starting to brown around the edges.

3 Once ready, arrange the roasted vegetables on a large serving dish, crumble over the goat's cheese and scatter the pine nuts on top. Garnish with parsley and serve at room temperature with the bread for mopping up the juices.

Frittata di maccheroni
Baked frittata with pasta, sun-dried tomatoes and parmesan

For those of you, who find traditional macaroni cheese too heavy, this alternative has that delicious crusty topping we all love but it's much lighter in taste and consistency. The eggs do the job of combining the ingredients and the sun-dried tomatoes and Parmesan are a heavenly combination.

Serves 4

509 cals	23.8g fat	6.6g saturates	4.4g sugar	1.3g salt

250g dried penne rigate

4 large eggs

75g sun-dried tomatoes in oil, drained and chopped

100g frozen peas, defrosted

60g freshly grated Parmesan cheese

3 tablespoons olive oil

Salt and freshly ground black pepper

1 Cook the pasta in boiling salted water until al dente, stirring every minute or so. To get the al dente perfect bite, cook the pasta for 1 minute less than indicated in the packet instructions. Drain the pasta in a colander and rinse immediately under cold water to stop the pasta cooking. Once cold, leave on the side to odrain for 5 minutes. Give the pasta a good shake every minute or two so that it doesn't stick.

2 Break the eggs into a large bowl and add in the sun-dried tomatoes, peas and grated Parmesan. Season with salt and pepper and mix everything together. Add the pasta to the egg mixture, mix well and leave to rest for 2 minutes. Preheat the oven to 190°C/gas mark 5.

3 Meanwhile, pour the oil into a 22cm diameter baking dish with sides about 5cm deep, ensuring that the dish is well coated with oil all around. Pour in the pasta mixture and spread out so that it is levelled up beautifully.

4 Cook in the middle of the oven for 20 minutes until crispy and set. Remove from the oven and allow the frittata to rest for 2 minutes before portioning. Serve warm.

Tip

Take advantage of your lunch break by walking around the block or park, rain or shine! A 15 minute walk at a fast pace will burn around 100 calories.

Pollo all'arancia e sciroppo
Maple syrup and orange-glazed chicken

I put this dish in this section because although I have suggested eating it hot with my lentil and walnut salad, having it cold with any kind of salad is still delicious. Simply slice the chicken breast and toss it with any green leaves – the sweetness of the maple syrup with the mustard and paprika will make it a perfect chicken salad. You may want to be more creative with what you serve with it, but do try and pair it with simple flavours to ensure the chicken remains the star of the plate.

Serves 4

207 cals	2.2g fat	0.5g saturates	9.5g sugar	2.3g salt

4 medium skinless, boneless chicken breasts

3 tablespoons maple syrup

1 tablespoon wholegrain mustard

Grated zest of 1 unwaxed orange

1 tablespoon dark soy sauce

1 teaspoon smoked paprika

1 teaspoon salt

1 Using a sharp knife, slash each chicken breast four times, cutting through to the middle of the breast. Tip the remaining ingredients in a large mixing bowl and mix everything together. Add the chicken to the marinade and turn to coat evenly. Cover with clingfilm and place in the fridge to marinate for 24 hours.

2 Take the chicken breasts out of the fridge 30 minutes before cooking them. Preheat a griddle pan to very hot. Cook the chicken for 5 minutes on each side, turning once and brushing over any remaining marinade.

3 Serve the chicken hot with my Lentil, Sun-dried Tomato and Walnut Salad (see page 80).

Pollo e costolette piccanti
Spicy sticky chicken and ribs

I have never met anyone who doesn't like barbecued food, and who says that it's only for summer? With this recipe, you can get those barbie flavours from roasting it in the oven in the comfort of your home instead of standing in the rain over coals. I serve this dish with salad, rice or jacket potatoes but if you're taking it to work for lunch, try it with a couscous salad. My one suggestion is to take some wipes as your fingers and lips will definitely get sticky.

Serves 6

278 cals	**9.9g** fat	**2.9g** saturates	**12.6g** sugar	**1.3g** salt

12 medium pork spare ribs
12 chicken pieces
250ml apple juice
4 tablespoons maple syrup
1 tablespoon olive oil
2 tablespoons dark soy sauce
1 teaspoon chilli powder
8 garlic cloves, unpeeled

1 Place the ribs and chicken pieces in a large roasting dish. Pour over all the ingredients, squelching everything together with your fingers to ensure the flavours are well combined. Cover the dish with clingfilm and leave to marinate in the fridge for 5 hours. Every 2 hours mix everything together again and continue to marinate in the fridge.

2 Remove the dish from the fridge and bring the meat to room temperature. Discard the clingfilm and ensure that the chicken pieces are skin-side up. Preheat the oven to 200°C/gas mark 6.

3 Roast the meat for 70 minutes. After the first 40 minutes, mix everything together and continue to cook. Serve hot with your favourite side salad and use any leftovers for your lunch box the following day.

Carpaccio di manzo con finocchio
Beef carpaccio with parmesan, fennel and chilli oil

I absolutely love this recipe. I'm a huge lover of steak and often make steak tartare but here I wanted to come up with something a bit different that incorporates strong flavours. I did this using chilli, Parmesan and fennel and, even if I say so myself, it's a great dish. If you prepare this the night before and take it into work for lunch the next day, the smell is enough to give everyone food envy, let alone how it looks and tastes. This also makes a fantastic starter; it takes no time to prepare but tastes very impressive.

Serves 4

| 521 | cals | 27g | fat | 7.9g | saturates | 3g | sugar | 1.4g | salt |

450g fillet of beef

3 tablespoons extra virgin olive oil

3 tablespoons freshly squeezed lemon juice

1 fennel bulb, finely sliced

50g freshly shaved Parmesan cheese

Grated zest of 1 unwaxed orange

2 tablespoons chilli-flavoured olive oil

12 thin slices of toasted ciabatta bread

Salt

1 Cut the beef into very thin slices and place between two sheets of clingfilm. Use a cooking mallet to gently bat out the slices into very thin slivers. Arrange the meat on a large serving dish.

2 Mix the olive oil with the lemon juice and a couple of pinches of salt. Drizzle over the meat and leave to marinate for 10 minutes at room temperature.

3 Scatter the fennel, Parmesan and orange zest over the meat. Finally drizzle over the chilli oil and serve immediately accompanied with toasted bread, or cover and chill in the fridge to eat the following day.

Insalata di polipo
Spicy octopus salad

This recipe brings back such happy memories because my grandfather always used to cook octopus for me; the smell alone takes me back to his house. In the south of Italy, where I'm from, eating seafood is an almost daily occurrence.

Serves 4

489 cals	22.7g fat	3.5g saturates	1.5g sugar	1.9g salt

1 octopus, weighing about 1kg

50ml extra virgin olive oil

2 teaspoons whole black peppercorns

1 teaspoon sea salt

2 garlic cloves, finely sliced

3 tablespoons chopped flat leaf parsley

Zest and juice of ½ unwaxed lemon

½ teaspoon dried chilli flakes

8 thin slices of toasted ciabatta bread, to serve

Salt

1 Preheat the oven to 110°C/gas mark ¼. To clean the octopus, turn the body pouch inside out and pull away the entrails and bone-like strips sticking to the side. Cut away the stomach sac, which is about the size of an avocado stone. Wash the octopus inside and out and then turn the body right-side out again. Press the beak and the soft surround out from the centre of the tentacles, cut away and discard.

2 Place the octopus into a small lidded casserole dish with half the oil, the peppercorns and sea salt. Cover with a lid and cook in the oven for 2 hours. Remove the dish from the oven and lift the octopus onto a plate to cool. Strain the cooking juices in a small saucepan and boil over a high heat until reduced by half. Set aside to cool, along with the octopus.

3 Cut off the tentacles and slice each one into diagonal slices about ½cm thick. Cut the body into similar size pieces. Put the prepared octopus in a large bowl and pour over 4 tablespoons of the reduced cooking liquor. Add in the garlic, half of the parsley, lemon zest and juice and the remaining extra virgin olive oil. Sprinkle over the chilli flakes with a pinch of salt and mix everything together.

4 Serve on a large serving platter, sprinkled with the remaining parsley, and accompanied with the toasted bread.

Tonno, fagioli e radicchio bianco
Beans, tuna and roasted chicory salad

I have to say that chicory is my vegetable of the year. I love them and am eating them roasted with a meat or fish dish at least once a week so I really wanted to incorporate them with one of my favourite salads of all time, the classic tuna and bean salad. Chicory's bitter flavour with the creamy butter beans and sweet tuna is amazing and will leave you wanting more. This salad is good for you in every way, giving you carbs, protein and vitamins in abundance, leaving you feeling ready to go. You'll probably be wanting to make another batch for tomorrow.

Serves 4

| 391 cals | 16.3g fat | 2.7g saturates | 4.7g sugar | 1.1g salt |

4 chicory

5 tablespoons extra virgin olive oil

1 x 400g can red kidney beans, drained

1 x 400g can butter beans, drained

1 red onion, peeled and finely sliced

Juice of ½ a lemon

2 tablespoons chopped flat-leaf parsley

2 x 200g cans tuna in brine or springwater, drained

Salt and freshly ground black pepper

4 thin slices of ciabatta bread, toasted

1 Preheat the oven to 190°C/gas mark 5. Place the chicory on a chopping board and halve lengthways. Transfer to a baking tray, drizzle over 2 tablespoons of the olive oil and season with salt and pepper. Transfer the tray to the middle of the oven and roast for 45 minutes.

2 Remove the tray from the oven and allow the chicory to cool at room temperature. Place the chicory on a chopping board and roughly chop into 2cm pieces. Set aside.

3 Place the drained beans in a large bowl with the sliced onions. Squeeze in the lemon juice from pour in the remaining oil. Add in the parsley and season with salt and pepper. Mix everything together and leave to rest for 10 minutes at room temperature, stirring occasionally.

4 Gently fold the tuna and roasted chicory into the bean salad and serve with the toasted ciabatta.

Insalatina di carote e menta
Carrot salad with mint and honey

I have to be honest with you here, I used to serve this dish hot as an accompaniment, but coming home very late one night, starving hungry (and a bit worse for wear), I opened the fridge and took out the first bowl I saw. It was my carrot recipe from the night before and I was in heaven. It tasted even better as a salad and I've been making it this way ever since. For a sweeter flavour, you might like to add raisins.

Serves 4

| 142 | cals | 6g | fat | 1g | saturates | 20.6g | sugar | 0.2g | salt |

700g medium carrots, trimmed

½ garlic clove, finely chopped

2 tablespoons runny honey

2 tablespoons white wine vinegar

2 tablespoons extra virgin olive oil

1 tablespoon finely shredded mint leaves

Salt and freshly ground black pepper

1 Fill a large saucepan at least three-quarters full with water. Add 2 tablespoons of salt and bring to the boil. Peel and halve the carrots lengthways then chop into half-moon shapes, each about 1cm thick.

2 Drop the carrots into the boiling water and cook for 7 minutes until just tender. Drain well and leave to cool slightly. Place the warm carrots in a large bowl with the remaining ingredients and mix everything together. Check the seasoning.

3 Serve at room temperature or take it to the office the next day.

Energy kicks

Barrette croccanti
My morning bars with pistachio and cranberries

Have you ever read the back of a cereal bar wrapper? In many cases, you will be hugely surprised to see that you are actually not being as good as you may think. Once I showed my wife that the 'healthy' bar she was eating contained as many calories and the same amount of fat as an ordinary chocolate bar or two packets of crisps. It pays to know what's in your food or, even better, make your own so you can be sure. This recipe is tasty, healthy and very quick and easy to make. The bars will last a week if kept in a sealed plastic container. You can vary the nuts and fruit as you like.

Makes 14 bars

| 139 cals | 4.6g fat | 0.5g saturates | 15.6g sugar | 0g salt |

150g dried cranberries
100g dried apricots
60g shelled pistachio nuts
50g sunflower seeds
50g porridge oats
60g wholemeal flour
60ml orange juice
4 tablespoons runny honey

1 Preheat the oven to 190°C/gas mark 5 and line a baking tray with greaseproof paper. Place the dried fruits in a food processor and blitz until roughly chopped.

2 Fold in the pistachio nuts, sunflower seeds, oats and flour. Pour in the orange juice with the honey and blitz again until roughly combined. Transfer the mixture to the prepared baking tray and spread out evenly with a knife until it is about 1cm thick.

3 Bake in the middle of the oven for 20 minutes until golden brown. Remove from the oven, leave to cool on the tray then slice into bars.

Cantuccini con pistacchio
Classic Italian double baked biscuits

Cantuccini are traditionally from Tuscany but every Italian region has its own recipe. In Naples, where I come from, we often prefer using pistachio nuts instead of almonds. Coffee and cantuccini are a match made in heaven and you will hardly ever be served an espresso in a bar in Italy without getting one of these delectable little biscuits on the side. Cantuccini always remind me of home – I will never tire of them.

Makes about 18

155	cals	6.1g	fat	0.9g	saturates	9.8g	sugar	0.1g	salt

170g shelled pistachio nuts
270g plain '00' white flour
150g caster sugar
1 teaspoon baking powder
2 large eggs, beaten
2 teaspoons vanilla extract
Zest of 1 unwaxed orange
Icing sugar for dusting

1 Preheat the oven to 180°C/gas mark 4 and line a large baking tray with baking paper. Tip the pistachio nuts into a medium bowl and pour over boiling water from the kettle. Leave them to soak for 2 minutes then drain and peel off the skins. Set aside.

2 Sift the flour, sugar and baking powder into a large mixing bowl. Stir in the pistachio nuts with the eggs, vanilla extract and orange zest and mix to form a biscuit dough. Dust the work surface with icing sugar, divide the dough into 3 pieces and shape each piece into a sausage by rolling it with your hands in icing sugar.

3 Place the rolls on the prepared baking tray and flatten slightly. Transfer the tray to the middle of the oven and bake for 20 minutes. Remove from the oven and place the rolls on a chopping board. Use a sharp knife to cut each roll diagonally into 1cm strips.

4 Spread out the strips in a single layer on the baking tray and return to the oven for 3 minutes. (You may need an extra baking tray.) Leave the cantuccini to cool on a wire rack before serving with a cup of strong coffee.

Anelli all'Amaretto con noccioline
Hazelnut and Amaretto rings

Many cake or biscuit recipes using hazelnuts come from the Piemonte region in northwest Italy but this particular one is my own creation. Lots of biscuits have flavours combined before they are baked but I wanted to try layering the biscuit so that it not only looks more decorative but means you get to taste the flavours together or one by one. Go ahead: eat in one, or lick the top of it first – whatever turns you on!

Makes 20

160	cals	9.1g	fat	4.8g	saturates	9.7g	sugar	0.1g	salt

180g salted butter at room temperature, plus extra for greasing

50g caster sugar

230g plain white flour, sifted

1 tablespoon skimmed milk

120g icing sugar, sifted

2 tablespoons Amaretto liqueur

50g unskinned hazelnuts, finely chopped

1 Preheat the oven to 180°C/gas mark 4 and grease a large baking tray with a little butter. Put the butter and caster sugar in a large mixing bowl and beat until pale and creamy. Using a wooden spoon, stir in the flour and milk to create fairly soft dough. (You may need to add a little more milk.)

2 Place the mixture into a piping bag fitted with a 1cm star nozzle. Pipe the mixture onto the greased baking tray to form rings 5cm in diameter, ensuring that the rings are spaced at least 3cm apart. Transfer the tray to the middle of the oven and bake for 10 minutes until golden.

3 Remove from the oven and transfer the biscuits to a wire rack to cool slightly. Place the icing sugar in a small bowl and pour in enough Amaretto to make a thin icing. Brush the icing over the still warm biscuits.

4 Sprinkle the chopped hazelnuts all over the biscuits and allow to set before serving. Perfect served with your favourite cup of tea.

Dolcetti al cioccolato
Chocolate brownies with Amaretto

In my previous book I created an amazing coffee and chocolate brownie. Someone told me off for it, as she said it was heaven but wished it wasn't so fattening – well, chocolate brownie lady, I love a challenge and this is for you: I hope you enjoy it. You will get all the brownie flavour without feeling guilty. Add some crushed nuts if you like a crunchier texture.

Makes 9 brownies

146	cals	5g	fat	2.5g	saturates	10.3g	sugar	0.5g	salt

2 tablespoons butter for greasing
2 egg whites
70g soft brown sugar
120g self-raising white flour
4 tablespoons cocoa powder
½ teaspoon baking powder
2 pinches of salt
2 medium eggs, beaten
4 tablespoons Amaretto liqueur

1 Preheat the oven to 190°C/gas mark 5. Grease the base and sides of an 18cm square baking tin. Whisk the egg whites in a large, clean mixing bowl until stiff. Gradually add in the sugar and continue to whisk until glossy.

2 Sift the flour, cocoa powder, baking powder and salt into a separate large mixing bowl. Beat the eggs and Amaretto into the dry ingredients. Gently fold in the whisked egg whites.

3 Spoon the mixture into the greased tin, level the surface, and transfer to the middle of the oven to bake for 18 minutes.

4 Leave the brownie to cool in the tin before turning it out and cutting into 9 squares. Delicious with a cup of your favourite coffee.

Carpaccio di arance con cioccolato
Orange salad with chocolate and pomegranate

If you have a sweet tooth but want to be healthy, here's the perfect recipe: fresh fruit with a little chocolate fix at the same time. As well as being delicious, oranges and pomegranates are packed with revitalising Vitamin C. To be honest, when they are in season, you can omit the icing sugar as the fruit are juicy and tasty enough; either way, you'll love the flavour and feel great too! Dark chocolate contains the antioxidant flavanol, which also has health benefits not found in milk or white chocolate.

Serves 4

194	cals	2.5g	fat	1.3g	saturates	40.8g	sugar	0.1g	salt

6 large oranges
2 tablespoons icing sugar
½ teaspoon ground cinnamon
Seeds from ½ pomegranate
20g piece of dark chocolate
   (minimum 70% cocoa solids)

1 Place the oranges on a chopping board and use a sharp, thin-bladed knife to slice off the top and bottom of each one. Then, cutting from the top down to the bottom, carefully slice away all the skin and white pith. Turn each orange on its side and cut into round slices, about ½cm thick.

2 Arrange the slices, overlapping, on a wide, shallow serving plate and sprinkle with the icing sugar. Cover with clingfilm and rest in the fridge for 45 minutes.

3 Just before serving, sprinkle the cinnamon over the oranges and scatter the pomegranate seeds on top. Finally grate the chocolate over the orange carpaccio and serve

Did you know?
Italy has the lowest intake of sugar and sugary foods in the whole of Europe – just 20g a day. That's roughly three small squares of chocolate.

Pere cotte
Pears poached with blackberries and apple juice

This poached dessert is so full of flavours everyone will definitely want seconds without realising they're being healthy eating it. You can add in a dash of liqueur if you like a kick and you can also make it with blueberries or raspberries if you prefer.

Serves 4

202	cals	1.2g	fat	0.5g	saturates	45.2g	sugar	0.1g	salt

4 medium pears

Zest of 1 unwaxed lemon, removed using a potato peeler

1 tablespoon freshly squeezed lemon juice

250g blackberries

250ml apple juice, unsweetened

50g caster sugar

8 tablespoons low-fat natural yogurt, to serve

1 Peel the pears but leave the stalks intact. Place in a medium saucepan with the lemon zest and juice. Add in half the blackberries, the apple juice and sugar. Heat until simmering, then cover the pan and cook gently for 25 minutes until the pears are tender, turning them once during cooking.

2 Remove the pears from the liquid using a slotted spoon and set aside cool on a plate for 5 minutes. Halve each pear and core using a teaspoon. Transfer 2 halves to the middle of 4 serving plates.

3 Strain the liquid through a sieve into a small pan. Add in the remaining blackberries and simmer gently for 4 minutes.

4 Pour the blackberry sauce all over the halved pears and serve with a little yogurt on top.

Tip

To strengthen your abs, lower back, improve balance and prevent energy slumps at work, try sitting on a fitness ball instead of an ordinary chair – it's a great way to work your core muscles. Sit with your weight balanced in the middle, hips pointing straight ahead, to keep your spine and lower back in alignment.

Marmellata di fragole e aceto balsamico
Strawberry and balsamic vinegar jam

I can't tell you how excited you will feel making your own jam. The first time you spread some on your toast gives you a sense of real satisfaction. Homemade jam also makes such a lovely present–when was the last time you received a jar? This unusual-sounding combination is strawberry with a kick and it's our favourite at home by far.

Makes 4 × 300ml jars

26	cals	0g	fat	0g	saturates	6.4g	sugar	0g	salt

3kg strawberries, hulled
Juice of 2 lemons
300g caster sugar
5 tablespoons balsamic vinegar

1 Preheat the oven to 200°C/gas mark 6. Wash the strawberries and dry them in a clean tea towel. Put the strawberries in a large ovenproof dish and drizzle over the lemon juice. Mix well and transfer the dish to the oven to bake for 25 minutes, stirring the strawberries with a wooden spoon halfway through cooking. Remove the dish from the oven and set aside to cool slightly.

2 Transfer the strawberries to a food processor and blitz to a purée. Return the purée to the dish and stir in the sugar and balsamic vinegar. Return the dish to the oven and cook for a further 30 minutes, stirring every 10 minutes.

3 Meanwhile, wash and sterilise four jars and lids in a dishwasher. Place them in the oven for 2 minutes to warm up; this will prevent the glass from cracking when hot jam is poured into them. Remove the jam from the oven and immediately pour it into the jars, allowing a 2cm gap at the top of each jar. Screw the lids on tightly.

4 Lay a cloth on the bottom of a medium saucepan and place the jars on top. Pour in enough warm water to completely cover the jars. If the jars don't fill the pan, wrap a cotton tea towel around them to stop them clattering against one another. Bring the water to the boil then simmer for 15 minutes.

5 Turn off the heat and let the jars to cool to room temperature before removing them from the water. At this point the lids are sucked in and a vacuum has formed. Dry the jars and store them in a cupboard away from direct light. Once opened, keep in the fridge and eat within a week.

Zabaglione al Marsala
Zabaglione served with Savoiardi biscuits

Zabaglione is one of the oldest Italian desserts that can be traced right back to the 16th century. In fact, you could argue that it was the first step towards making ice cream. Florence and Sicily are still battling out which region originally concocted the recipe but I'm just glad someone did. It's a simple dessert yet I promise your guests will feel you've really spoilt them.

Serves 4

264	cals	8.6g	fat	2.5g	saturates	28.4g	sugar	0.1g	salt

250ml Marsala wine
80g caster sugar
5 egg yolks
4 Savoiardi biscuits,
  to serve

1 Pour the Marsala wine into a medium saucepan and heat gently until reduced by half. Set aside to cool, then stir in 20g of the sugar. Place the egg yolks and the remaining sugar into a heatproof glass bowl and beat using an electric whisk for about 5 minutes until thick and pale yellow.

2 Place the bowl over a small saucepan of barely simmering water (do not allow the bowl to be in contact with the water) and continue to whisk for a further 12 minutes, gradually drizzling in the Marsala wine. The egg mixture should almost triple in volume, hold soft peaks and have a light, foamy texture. It's important not to allow the egg mixture to become too hot or it will start to cook around the edges of the bowl and lose volume.

3 Spoon the zabaglione into 4 tall glasses and serve warm with the Savoiardi biscuits.

Gelato allo yogurt con mango
Mango and vanilla ice yogurt

I know I'm biased, but for me, you can't get better-flavoured ice cream anywhere in the world than in Italy. So how, well might you ask, am I going to come up with a delicious ice cream using no sugar or cream? Low fat natural yogurt with sweet fresh mangoes will taste just as good – trust me, I'm Italian!!

Serves 4

202 cals	1.8g fat	1.1g saturates	37.4g sugar	2.5g salt

500g ripe mangoes, peeled, stoned and cut into small cubes

3 tablespoons maple syrup

Grated zest and juice of 1 unwaxed lime

2 teaspoons vanilla extract

600ml low-fat natural yogurt

1 Place all the ingredients in a food processor and blitz for 30 seconds until smooth. Transfer the mixture to a freezer container with a tight-fitting lid and freeze for 1 hour.

2 Remove from the freezer and whisk well with a fork to break up the ice crystals. Freeze for a further hour.

3 Repeat the process 3 times before freezing the mixture completely. (The more times you whisk the yogurt ice while it is freezing, the smoother it will be.)

4 Serve my mango ice yogurt with a selection of fresh fruits.

Noccioline speziate al forno
Roasted nuts Italian-style

Nuts are so good for you, being not only full of healthy fats, vitamins and protein but incredibly good for your heart, helping to keep your arteries clear. They make a great choice for a snack as they really keep hunger pangs at bay, and this recipe is fantastic as a nibble at parties. Serving a selection of nuts baked in this spicy marinade is just *fantastico*!

Serves 10

234	cals	22.2g	fat	2.4g	saturates	1.5g	sugar	0.5g	salt

1 teaspoon smoked paprika

½ teaspoon garlic powder

½ teaspoon ground coriander

½ teaspoon chilli powder

1 tablespoon fresh rosemary
leaves, finely chopped

1 teaspoon salt

100g cashew nuts

100g pecan nuts

100g hazelnuts

50g almonds

1 tablespoon olive oil

1 Preheat the oven to 200° C/gas mark 6. Place all the spices, rosemary and salt in a medium bowl. Pour in 1 tablespoon of water and mix with a fork to make a paste. Add the nuts to the paste and mix everything together until the nuts are evenly coated.

2 Grease a roasting tin with the oil and tip in the nuts. Transfer the tin to the middle of the oven and roast for 10 minutes. Stir the nuts and continue to roast for a further 5 minutes. Remove from the oven and allow the spiced nuts to cool in the tin.

3 Enjoy the nuts immediately or keep them in an airtight container for a few days.

Tip

A pre-workout coffee will not only help to boost performance – research in the *International Journal Of Sports Nutrition* has shown that it can boost fat burning by up to 30%, too, and increase the amount of calories you will burn after exercise.

Quick meals

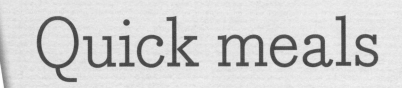

Insalata di zucchine e noci
Courgette and walnut salad with balsamic glaze

I quite often lightly grill courgettes to make a similar salad but one day I was cooking myself a steak and to be honest, just couldn't be bothered to grill my courgettes but at the same time, I really fancied some. I tried the same process but using raw slices of courgettes and couldn't believe how amazing they were. This recipe is great as a salad or an accompaniment and it couldn't be simpler to prepare. Try making it with carrots if you prefer. *Buon appetito.*

Serves 4

| 491 cals | 34.6g fat | 4.3g saturates | 11.6g sugar | 0.7g salt |

4 medium courgettes

80ml extra virgin olive oil

2 garlic cloves, finely chopped

70g walnut halves

60g rocket leaves

4 tablespoons ready-made
   balsamic glaze

Salt and freshly ground
   black pepper

8 thin slices of toasted ciabatta

1 Trim the ends off the courgettes then slice them lengthways into wafer-thin slices. (Using a potato peeler gives you perfect thin slices.) Transfer the slices into a large mixing bowl.

2 Pour over the oil with the garlic and walnuts, season with salt and pepper and mix all together. Leave to marinate in the fridge for 20 minutes.

3 Transfer the marinated courgettes onto a large serving plate and scatter over the rocket leaves. Drizzle over the balsamic glaze and set aside for 5 minutes before serving.

4 Serve my courgette salad at room temperature accompanied with toasted ciabatta bread.

Lenticchie e noci

Lentils, sun-dried tomatoes and walnut salad

You really don't often find the humble lentil on many menus and yet it is such a great type of bean and readily absorbs a variety of flavours. One of the oldest, most nutritious pulses that have been part of our history and culture for over 8,000 years, lentils are really easy to cook and full of protein. This salad is perfect as a starter for four sharing off one plate but can also be used an accompaniment for fish or meat.

Serves 4

| 419 | cals | 23.2g | fat | 2.5g | saturates | 5.5g | sugar | 2g | salt |

1 x 400g can lentils, drained and rinsed

2 tablespoons chopped flat-leaf parsley

60g walnut pieces

150g sun-dried tomatoes in oil, drained and finely sliced

2 tablespoons walnut oil

1 tablespoon sherry vinegar

8 thin slices of toasted ciabatta bread

2 garlic cloves, peeled

Salt and freshly ground black pepper

1 Put the lentils in a medium bowl with the parsley, walnuts and sun-dried tomatoes. Pour over the walnut oil and the vinegar. Season with salt and pepper and mix everything together. Set aside for a couple of minutes.

2 Lightly rub both sides of the toasted ciabatta with the garlic. Pile the lentil salad in the middle of a large serving plate and serve with the toasted ciabatta.

Bruschette con crema d'avocado
Avocado and smoked paprika bruschette

Believe it or not, I tasted my first avocado when I came to England and, contrary to the popularity of 'Tricolore salad' in Britain, in Italy, this dish just doesn't exist. On its own, avocado can often be bland but it's fantastic in salads or with a spicy dish. I wanted to create a recipe with this fruit, as it has an extremely high nutritional value and helps provide many general health benefits. As well as being a source of vitamin E and monounsaturated fat, avocado is one of the best sources of glutathione, a molecule which help to burn off fat in the body, and also helps prevent many diseases, including several forms of cancer, heart disease, diabetes and cholesterol.

Serves 4

396 cals	23g fat	4.6g saturates	5.8g sugar	1.1g salt

3 ripe avocados

4 teaspoons freshly squeezed lime juice

4 x 2cm thick slices of rustic bread, halved and toasted

1 teaspoon smoked paprika

4 large round tomatoes, cut into ½ cm slices, to serve

Salt

1 Halve the avocados, discard the stone and scoop the flesh into a medium bowl. Pour over the lime juice and mash roughly using a fork. Season with salt.

2 Spread the avocado mixture on each toasted piece of bread and sprinkle with a little paprika.

3 Serve accompanied with a few slices of tomatoes, and enjoy with a cold Italian beer.

Cavolo nero, aglio olio e peperoncino
Cavolo nero with garlic, oil and chilli

Cavolo Nero, a type of curly kale, is typical Tuscan produce. This loose-leaf cabbage is dark green – almost black – hence its name, *nero* meaning black in Italian. This little gem is a great source of iron, calcium, vitamin C, vitamin K and folic acid but more importantly, it tastes great and is a great alternative to the more familiar broccoli which we're probably bored with. Try this recipe: I know you'll love it!

Serves 4

254 cals	24g fat	2.6g saturates	2.2g sugar	0.4g salt

1 whole head cavolo nero
2 tablespoons extra virgin olive oil
2 garlic cloves, peeled and sliced
½ teaspoon dried chilli flakes
80g crushed walnuts
Maldon salt

1 Bring a medium saucepan of salted water to the boil. Pull the leaves off the hard stalks of the cavolo nero and wash them under cold running water. Finely shred the leaves and cook in the boiling water for 5 minutes. Drain and set aside.

2 Heat the oil in a large frying pan and gently fry the garlic and chilli flakes for 30 seconds. Add the cooked cavolo nero with the walnuts, season with salt and fry for 5 minutes, stirring constantly with a wooden spoon. If the leaves are sticking to the pan, add a tablespoon of warm water.

3 Serve immediately to accompany a main course or cool to room temperature then store in a sealed container in the fridge for the day after. Do not keep longer than 48 hours and only reheat it once.

Tip

When you come home from work and haven't had a chance to exercise yet, avoid the couch like the plague. Slip on some trainers and get out there, even if it's only for a 10-minute walk.

Triglie al cartoccio
Baked red mullet with thyme and white wine

I love the authentic way this dish is served. Giving each person their own foil parcel to open seems so homely to me, and it means the delicious wine gravy remains around the fish. It's definitely rustic not fancy and yet feels special. I have chosen red mullet for its flavour and sheer good looks, but substitute snapper if you prefer. Serve with salad in a separate bowl in case any hot liquid seeps from the foil and cooks the leaves. Enjoy!

Serves 4

391	cals	25.2g	fat	2.6g	saturates	0.6g	sugar	0.6g	salt

4 whole red mullet, about 250g each, cleaned and scaled

1 small bunch of thyme

2 garlic cloves, peeled and halved

70ml extra virgin olive oil, plus extra for brushing

50ml dry white wine

8 tablespoons freshly squeezed lemon juice

Salt and freshly ground black pepper

1 Preheat the oven to 220°C/gas mark 7. Season the mullet with salt and pepper inside and out. Put 3 sprigs of thyme and half the garlic in the cavity of both fish. Prepare 4 × 30cm squares of foil. Brush with a little oil and put a fish diagonally across the centre of each piece. Bring up the sides of the foil around the fish and crimp it together tightly at each end, but leave the top part open.

2 Pour the wine into a medium bowl and mix in 50ml of cold water. Pour 2 tablespoons of the mixture into each foil parcel, together with 2 tablespoons of lemon juice and a quarter of the extra virgin olive oil.

3 Seal the parcels well and place on a baking tray. Transfer to the middle of the oven and bake for 10 minutes. To serve, transfer the unopened parcels to 4 warm serving plates and take them to the table, along with a bowl of crispy salad of your choice.

4 Allow your guests to open their own parcel and enjoy the mullet with a glass of dry white wine.

Tonno alla griglia con briciole
Grilled tuna steak with garlic breadcrumbs

Every now and then fish and chips in the UK is a must, but I must admit I often prefer my fish in breadcrumbs rather than batter – they make a far lighter coating that really means you taste the fish – and with this recipe I've come up with a much healthier but still delicious version. Tuna is such tasty meaty fish and the breadcrumbs add a bit of luxury to it. Serve with a crisp salad and a glass of wine.

Serves 4

| 432 cals | 17.4g fat | 3.4g saturates | 1.5g sugar | 0.8g salt |

Juice of 1 medium lemon

120g fresh breadcrumbs

2 garlic cloves, crushed to a purée

2 tablespoons freshly chopped flat-leaf parsley

1 teaspoon dry chilli flakes

3 tablespoons extra virgin olive oil

4 tuna steaks, about 180g each

Salt to taste

1 lemon, cut into 4 wedges, to serve

1 Preheat a griddle pan. Use your fingertips to mix together the lemon juice, breadcrumbs, garlic, parsley, chilli and oil in a medium bowl. If the mixture seems too wet, add more breadcrumbs.

2 Season the tuna steaks with salt and dip each side into the breadcrumbs mixture. Press down with your hands to ensure that the breadcrumbs coat the tuna evenly.

3 Cook on the hot griddle pan for 3 minutes on each side until brown and crispy all over. Place the tuna steaks on a chopping board and use a sharp knife to cut them in half.

4 Serve immediately with a wedge of lemon and some crunchy mixed salad – fantastic served with a glass of dry Italian white wine.

Tip

Short on time? Go faster and harder for better results. If you're running, increase speed; if you're working out on a machine, up the resistance. Studies show that even if you decrease the frequency and duration of exercise, you can still boost your fitness level by maintaining a high intensity. Or, you can divide your workout into three 10 to 15 minute sessions throughout the day.

Fusilli al pesto Genovese
Pasta with Genoese basil pesto

Pesto is the famous sauce from Genova in the Liguria region of northern Italy. There are many versions of this sauce but I have kept the traditional recipe in my book as it really is the easiest and quickest to create. The name pesto comes from the Italian word *pestare*, meaning to pound or crush, and refers to the original method of preparation using a pestle and mortar. This pesto is also amazing dolloped on baked cod or simply on baked jacket potato.

Serves 4

| 617 | cals | 34.8g | fat | 5.3g | saturates | 3.4g | sugar | 0.6g | salt |

50g basil leaves, stripped from the stems

50g pine nuts

1 garlic clove, peeled

90ml extra virgin olive oil

25g freshly grated Pecorino cheese

350g fusilli pasta

Salt and freshly ground black pepper

1 Put the basil, pine nuts and garlic in a food processor. Drizzle in the oil with 50ml of cold water and blitz until smooth. Transfer the basil mixture into a large bowl and fold in the Pecorino. Season with a little salt.

2 Fill a large saucepan at least three-quarters full with water. Add in 2 tablespoons of salt and bring to the boil. Cook the pasta in the boiling water until al dente, stirring every minute or so. To get the al dente perfect bite, cook the pasta for 1 minute less than indicated in the packet instructions. Drain and tip the pasta into the bowl with the pesto.

3 Toss everything together for 15 seconds to ensure the pasta is evenly coated with pesto. Serve immediately.

Penne al pomodoro
Pasta with basil and tomato sauce

This has to be the most popular Italian pasta dish of all time – especially with children – but I confess I always thoroughly enjoy it when I make it for myself; in fact I often use the kids as my excuse to make it, just so I can have some. It's so simple and easy to prepare yet full of flavour using very few ingredients. You can use fusilli or farfalle instead of penne, and of course top it with Parmesan cheese if you fancy. Do not use fresh tomatoes, though, otherwise the sauce will be too watery.

Serves 4

| 462 cals | 10.3g fat | 1g saturates | 11g sugar | 0.3g salt |

3 tablespoons extra virgin olive oil

1 medium onion, finely chopped

2 x 400g cans chopped tomatoes

8 basil leaves

400g dried penne rigate

Salt and freshly ground
    black pepper

1 Pour the oil into a medium saucepan over a low heat and fry the onions for about 3 minutes until golden, stirring with a wooden spoon. Add the tomatoes and basil, season with salt and pepper and cook, uncovered, over a medium heat for 10 minutes, stirring every 5 minutes.

2 Fill a large saucepan at least three-quarters full with water. Add in 2 tablespoons of salt and bring to the boil. Cook the pasta in the boiling water until al dente, stirring every minute or so. To get the al dente perfect bite, cook the pasta for 1 minute less than indicated in the packet instructions. Drain and return the pasta to the same pan away from the heat.

3 Pour over the tomato and basil sauce and stir everything together for 30 seconds to allow the flavours to combine. Serve immediately.

Gnocchi alla Caprese
Gnocchi with tomato, mozzarella and basil

There is a local Italian restaurant near our home with a fantastic chef called Pasquale where we often go as a family en route to or from a day out, and I don't think we've ever been there without my wife ordering Gnocchi alla Caprese. These delectable little potato dumplings are still not fully appreciated by the British palate even though I have never met anyone who doesn't like this dish and it definitely gets the thumbs up from children. If you prefer a little extra kick, drizzle over some chilli oil. I am dedicating this recipe to the owners of the restaurant: Nardo and Lorenzo, you guys are the best!

Serves 4

487	cals	21.6g	fat	9.8g	saturates	10.7g	sugar	2.8g	salt

3 tablespoons extra virgin olive oil

1 medium onion, finely chopped

700ml passata (sieved tomatoes)

10 fresh basil leaves

500g ready-made plain gnocchi

2 x 125g Mozzarella balls, drained and cut into 1cm cubes

Salt and freshly ground black pepper

1 Heat the oil in a large frying pan and fry the onion over a medium heat for about 3 minutes until golden. Pour in the passata and continue to cook for a further 10 minutes, stirring occasionally with a wooden spoon. Stir in the basil, season with salt and pepper and remove from the heat.

2 Meanwhile, fill a medium saucepan three-quarters full with water, add 1 tablespoon of salt and bring to the boil. Drop the gnocchi into the boiling salted water and cook just until they start to float to the top. Drain well and place in the frying pan with the tomato sauce.

3 Return the frying pan to a low heat and cook for 1 minute, stirring occasionally to allow the sauce to coat the gnocchi.

4 Scatter over the Mozzarella and continue to cook for a further 30 seconds allowing the cheese to slightly melt. Serve immediately.

Pollo alla pizzaiola
Chicken breasts in pizza sauce with melted mozzarella

Ok, you've had a really busy day but there's a family of hungry faces looking at you expectantly. You really can't be bothered and would sooner order take-away but you know that it won't taste as good as your home cooking. This is the recipe for you. It doesn't take long to prepare, offers everyone a healthy tasty meal and leaves you feeling pleased that your family has enjoyed a great meal made with ingredients you are bound to have in your cupboard. You can also make this with veal instead of chicken if you prefer.

Serves 4

| 454 cals | 25.6g fat | 10.6g saturates | 5.6g sugar | 1.2g salt |

4 medium skinless, boneless chicken breasts

4 tablespoons olive oil

3 garlic cloves, peeled and finely sliced

2 x 400g cans chopped tomatoes

1 teaspoon dried oregano

2 x 125g mozzarella balls, drained and finely sliced

Salt and freshly ground black pepper

1 Using a sharp knife, slash each chicken breast four times, cutting through to the middle of the breast. Heat the olive oil in a large frying pan and gently fry the garlic and the chicken over a medium heat for 2 minutes on each side until golden all over.

2 Pour in the chopped tomatoes and oregano and season with salt and pepper. Cook uncovered over a medium heat for 8 minutes. Half-way through the cooking, turn the chicken breasts. Meanwhile, preheat the grill to its highest setting.

3 Remove the pan from the heat and place the sliced mozzarella on top of the chicken breasts. Grind over some black pepper and place the pan under the grill for about 1 minute or until the cheese starts to melt. (Protect the handle of the frying pan with foil, if necessary.)

4 To serve, pour some of the tomato sauce in the middle of 4 serving plates, top with a chicken breast and enjoy with some warm crusty bread.

Tagliata di manzo con pesto
Sliced steak with rocket leaves and pesto dressing

This recipe is dedicated to my eldest son, Luciano. He is the most amazing eater I have ever known, enjoying most food from snails to rocket leaf and he's always willing to try new things. He absolutely loves this recipe and not many ten-year-olds would prefer it with salad than chips – he really does me proud. If you prefer, dress the salad with a simple balsamic vinaigrette and you can use fillet steak for a softer cut of meat. Please, please, please don't overcook the meat, otherwise it will be tough.

Serves 4

| 430 | cals | 23.1g | fat | 7.1g | saturates | 2.8g | sugar | 0.9g | salt |

4 sirloin steaks, about 200g each, fat removed

2 tablespoons extra virgin olive oil, plus a little extra to oil the steaks

3 tablespoons good-quality basil pesto (shop-bought is fine)

150g rocket leaves

20 cherry tomatoes, washed and halved

Freshly shaved Parmesan cheese

Salt and freshly ground black pepper

1 Preheat a griddle pan to very hot. Rub the steaks with a little oil and make little cuts along the trimmed edge of the meat to prevent it shrinking and curving as it cooks. Cook on the griddle pan for 2 minutes on each side for medium cooked steak. (Add an extra 2 minutes on each side if you prefer your meat well done.)

2 Season with salt and pepper and transfer the steaks to a chopping board to rest for 1 minute, covered with foil to keep them warm.

3 Pour the pesto in a small bowl with the extra virgin olive oil and 3 tablespoons of warm water. Whisk together and set aside. Tip the rocket leaves and the tomatoes into a large bowl, pour in half of the pesto dressing, season with salt and pepper and mix well using your fingertips. Pile up the rocket salad in the middle of 4 serving plates.

4 Using a long sharp knife, cut the steaks on the diagonal into 1cm slices and lay on the rocket salad. Drizzle over the remaining pesto dressing and scatter the Parmesan shavings on top. Serve immediately with a cold Italian beer.

Pesche affogate al vino rosso
Fresh peaches in red wine with vanilla ice cream

I used to have a house in Sardinia where we went every summer and I remember making this peach recipe each morning ready for the evening. My friends and I would sit on the terrace after a barbecue and salad and enjoy eating the peaches, drinking the wine and soaking up the views. I tried to reinvent the moment in the UK but sitting at our dining table, staring out at the rain, wasn't really the same so I added in a scoop of ice cream and somehow it softened the blow. This is a great dessert and quick to put together.

Serves 4

318	cals	3.3g	fat	1.8g	saturates	55.6g	sugar	0.1g	salt

800g ripe, white flesh peaches

350ml Italian red wine

110g caster sugar

4 scoops low-fat vanilla ice cream

1 Peel the peaches and cut in half. Remove the stone, cut each half into quarters and place in a large bowl. Pour over the wine with sugar and gently fold everything together. Leave to chill in the fridge for at least 1 hour, to allow the flavours to combine.

2 Divide the peaches between 4 dessert glasses and pour over any wine remaining in the bowl. Arrange a ball of ice cream on top and serve immediately.

Affogato al caffe
Ice cream with hot espresso and Cointreau

This is one of my favourite desserts of all time – I have it at least twice a week at home. It takes seconds to prepare, is totally delicious and finishes off any meal perfectly. You can omit the Cointreau if you prefer. I have tried this with other flavoured ice creams but for me, vanilla is the only way to go. Enjoy.

Serves 4

224	cals	8.5g	fat	1.5g	saturates	23.1g	sugar	0g	salt

400g low-fat vanilla ice cream

4 shots freshly made espresso coffee

4 tablespoons Cointreau liqueur

2 chocolate flakes, crushed

1 Drop 2 scoop of vanilla ice cream into each of 4 stemmed glasses or cappuccino cups.

2 Pour a shot of freshly made hot espresso over each serving, followed by 1 tablespoon of Cointreau.

3 Sprinkle with crushed chocolate flakes and serve immediately.

Dinner for two

Carpaccio di tonno con rucola e Parmigiano

Tuna carpaccio with rocket and parmesan

I often make this dish as a starter as it's light yet full of flavour, and I've included it here as I feel there is something really romantic about it. It's fresh, simple yet somehow really elegant. No one will even notice they are being 'good' and your guest will feel as if you have really gone out of your way to conjure up something difficult; in reality, apart from the advance freezing, it takes seconds to prepare. Please don't leave the tuna in the freezer longer than instructed or it will be impossible to slice.

Serves 2

| 457 cals | 20.6g fat | 4.6g saturates | 2.2g sugar | 2.2g salt |

200g piece of tuna loin fillet

2 tablespoons extra virgin olive oil

15g Parmesan shavings

1 tablespoon little capers in vinegar, drained

30g rocket leaves

Sea salt and freshly ground black pepper

6 thin slices of ciabatta bread, toasted, to serve

1 Wrap the tuna tightly in clingfilm to create a nice cylindrical shape. Put it in the freezer to rest for about 3 hours until firm but not completely frozen solid. Meanwhile chill 2 flat serving plates in the fridge.

2 Remove the parcel from the freezer, unwrap it and place the tuna on a chopping board. Using a very sharp, long-bladed knife, cut across into very thin slices – aim to make them as thin as smoked salmon.

3 Arrange the tuna slices in a single layer over the base of the cold serving plates. Drizzle over the oil and then sprinkle with a little black pepper and sea salt.

4 Scatter the Parmesan shavings and capers over the tuna and pile the rocket leaves into the centre of each plate. Serve with the toasted ciabatta.

Pizza Scue' Scue'

Thin-crust pizza with mozzarella, cherry tomatoes and pesto

Margheritas are one of Italy's most famous pizzas but add just one ingredient and it's a whole new concept. The fresh taste of basil pesto really enhances all the original flavours but makes you feel that you have created something extra-special. You can't beat a scrumptious authentically made pizza that delivers all the traditional flavours with a twist – trust me, it's *fantastico!* Choose any topping you like but do try this recipe first, it won't disappoint.

Makes 2 pizzas

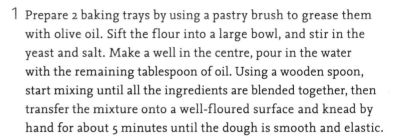

620 cals	30.2g fat	11.2g saturates	4.5g sugar	1.6g salt

170g strong plain flour, plus extra for dusting

7g (one sachet) fast-action dried yeast

Pinch of salt

120ml warm water

1 tablespoon extra virgin olive oil, plus extra for greasing

for the topping

200g cherry tomatoes, quartered

1 x 125g mozzarella balls, drained and cut into 1cm cubes

1 tablespoons basil pesto

1 tablespoon extra virgin olive oil

Salt and pepper

1 Prepare 2 baking trays by using a pastry brush to grease them with olive oil. Sift the flour into a large bowl, and stir in the yeast and salt. Make a well in the centre, pour in the water with the remaining tablespoon of oil. Using a wooden spoon, start mixing until all the ingredients are blended together, then transfer the mixture onto a well-floured surface and knead by hand for about 5 minutes until the dough is smooth and elastic.

2 Shape the dough into a ball and put back into the bowl. Brush the top with a little oil, cover with clingfilm and leave at room temperature to rest for 25 minutes. Preheat the oven to 200°C/ gas mark 6.

3 To prepare the topping, place the tomatoes and mozzarella in a large bowl. Add the oil and pesto, season with a little salt and pepper and mix everything together. Set aside at room temperature for 15 minutes, stirring every 5 minutes, to allow all the flavours to combine properly.

4 Once rested, turn out the dough onto a well-floured surface and divide it in half. Use your hands to push each one out from the centre to create 2 round discs about 25cm in diameter. Place the bases on the prepared baking trays.

5 Divide the tomato and mozzarella mixture between the 2 pizzas and drizzle over any remaining juices from the bowl. Transfer the trays to the middle of the oven and cook for 18 minutes, until golden and brown. Serve hot.

Pizza Vesuvio
The no. 1 spicy pizza

This recipe is for all you ladies to make for your partners, purely because I would love to have this made for me. After a hard day's work, coming home to a homemade spicy pizza and a cold glass of beer is absolute heaven. Just the smell of the spicy vegetables and salami, along with freshly made pizza dough makes your mouth water. Trust me, if you need to ask a favour from your partner make this first – it might not guarantee a yes but it will definitely enhance your chances!

Makes 1 large pizza

170g strong plain flour, plus extra for dusting

7g (one sachet) fast-action dried yeast

Pinch of salt

120ml warm water

1 tablespoon extra virgin olive oil, plus extra for greasing

for the topping

1 tablespoon extra virgin olive oil

1 large red pepper, halved, deseeded and cut into ½ cm strips

1 fresh red chilli, deseeded and finely chopped

½ large red onion, peeled and finely sliced

100g passata (sieved tomatoes)

1 teaspoon dried chilli flakes

1 x 125g mozzarella ball, drained and cut into 1cm cubes

4 slices Neapolitan salami

Salt

| 679 | cals | 31.1g | fat | 12.1g | saturates | 12.7g | sugar | 2.1g | salt |

1 First cook the vegetables for the topping. Pour 4 tablespoons of oil into a large frying pan over a medium heat. Fry the pepper, fresh chilli and onion for 8 minutes, stirring frequently. Season with salt, then set aside to cool. Prepare 2 baking trays by pouring 1 tablespoon of oil into each tray and spread it using your fingers or a pastry brush.

2 Sift the flour into a large bowl, and stir in the yeast and salt. Make a well in the centre, pour in the water with the remaining tablespoon of oil. Using a wooden spoon, start mixing until all the ingredients are blended together, then transfer the mixture onto a well-floured surface and knead by hand for about 5 minutes until the dough is smooth and elastic.

3 Shape the dough into a ball and put back into the bowl. Brush the top with a little oil, cover with clingfilm and leave at room temperature to rest for 25 minutes. Preheat the oven to 200°C/ gas mark 6.

4 Once rested, turn out the dough onto a well-floured surface and divide it in half. Use your hands to push each one out from the centre to create 2 round discs about 25cm in diameter. Place the bases on the prepared baking trays.

5 Spread the passata evenly over the pizza bases using the back of a tablespoon. Sprinkle over the chilli flakes and season with salt. Scatter the mozzarella and cooked vegetables over the 2 pizzas and top with the salami slices. Transfer the trays to the middle of the oven and cook for 18 minutes, until golden and brown. Serve hot.

Spaghetti alla ciociara
Pasta with ham, eggs and mushrooms

Some of you reading this recipe might wonder why I add egg yolks to the sauce. Easy – it's because they give it an amazing creamy texture without the need to use cream or mascarpone. Without some kind of tomato or creamy sauce the mushrooms and ham don't coat the spaghetti so well, but using eggs really works, allowing the main flavours to be the stars of the show, as intended. You can make this using linguine or tagliatelle and Parmesan is as good as Pecorino if you prefer. Please, please, please, ensure that you cook the pasta al dente.

Serves 2

602 cals	**26.2g** fat	**8.5g** saturates	**3.7g** sugar	**2.3g** salt

1 tablespoon extra virgin olive oil

10g salted butter

100g cubed lean ham

100g button mushrooms, sliced

180g spaghetti

3 large egg yolks, beaten

2 tablespoons freshly chopped flat-leaf parsley

10g freshly grated Pecorino Romano cheese

Salt and freshly ground black pepper

1 Heat the oil and the butter together in a large frying pan over a medium heat. Add the ham, mushrooms, a pinch of black pepper and fry for 8 minutes until crispy, stirring occasionally with a wooden spoon.

2 Fill a large saucepan at least three-quarters full with water. Add in 2 tablespoons of salt and bring to the boil. Cook the pasta in the boiling water until al dente, stirring every minute or so. To get the al dente perfect bite, cook the pasta for 1 minute less than indicated in the packet instructions. Drain and tip the pasta into the frying pan with the ham and mushrooms.

3 Remove the pan from the heat, stir in the egg yolks with the parsley and keep stirring for 30 seconds until you create a creamy texture. Season with salt (check carefully, as ham can be salty). Serve immediately with the grated cheese on top.

Did you know?

According to the International Pasta Organisation, Italians each eat, on average, 26kg of pasta a year. That's around three times more than Americans, six times as much as Australians and 10 times more than Brits!

Bucatini all'Amatriciana

Classic Roman pasta with tomatoes, pancetta and red onions

My best friend and business partner, Marco, stays over at least once a week – normally after a long day at work, He's from Rome and this recipe originates from Amatrice, northeast of Rome, so I often make it when he's around. It's really flavoursome and leaves you feeling full but without that heavy feeling some creamy sauces can cause. You will always have most of the ingredients in your cupboard and it's quick and easy to prepare. Substitute the Pecorino for Parmesan if you prefer and if you don't like bucatini, try linguine. *Buon Appetito.*

Serves 2

585	cals	23.4g	fat	8.2g	saturates	10.4g	sugar	2.2g	salt

1 tablespoon olive oil

1 small red onion, finely sliced
	teaspoon dried chilli flakes

75g diced pancetta

1 x 400g can chopped tomatoes

175g bucatini

2 tablespoons freshly chopped
	flat-leaf parsley

30g freshly grated Pecorino
	Romano

Salt to taste

1 Heat the oil in a large frying pan or wok and fry the onions over a medium heat for about 3 minutes, stirring occasionally with a wooden spoon. Add the chilli and the pancetta and continue to cook for a further 5 minutes, stirring occasionally. Pour in the chopped tomatoes, stir well and gently simmer, uncovered, for 5 minutes, stirring every couple of minutes. Season with salt, remove from the heat and set aside.

2 Meanwhile, cook the pasta in a large saucepan with plenty of boiling salted water until al dente. Drain and tip into the pan with the tomato sauce.

3 Return the frying pan to a medium heat, sprinkle over the parsley and gently stir everything together for 15 seconds to allow the flavours to combine. Serve immediately, sprinkled with Pecorino.

Tip

Exercise companions add a social element to any routine. Ask a friend or your partner to be your workout buddy – you won't skip a workout if someone is waiting for you.

Linguine ai frutti di mare
Seafood pasta with white wine and cherry tomatoes

This takes me back to being at home in my village, Torre del Greco. It is a traditional Neapolitan recipe and has to be my favourite pasta dish of all time. If, like me, you are a seafood lover, it doesn't get much better than this. My grandfather Giovanni always used to make this, and it was one of the first dishes I mastered. I would eat this daily if I could – and I often do when I go back home. Please ensure you buy fresh seafood from your local fishmonger and discard any unopened mussels or clams once cooked.

Serves 2

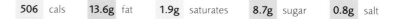

506 cals   **13.6g** fat   **1.9g** saturates   **8.7g** sugar   **0.8g** salt

100g clams

100g mussels

50ml dry white wine

2 tablespoons extra virgin olive oil

1 garlic clove, peeled and finely sliced

Pinch of dried chilli flakes

1 x 400g can cherry tomatoes

100g raw prawns, peeled with head and tail off

175g linguine

2 tablespoons chopped flat-leaf parsley

Zest of ½ unwaxed lemon

Salt to taste

1 Wash the clams and mussels under cold running water, discarding broken ones and any that do not close when tapped firmly. Place the shellfish in a large saucepan, pour in the wine, cover, and cook over a medium heat for 3 minutes, until all the shells have opened. Discard any that remain closed. Tip into a colander placed over a bowl and set aside.

2 Pour the oil into the same saucepan in which you cooked the clams and mussels and gently fry the garlic until it begins to sizzle. Add the chilli and the cherry tomatoes and cook over a medium heat for 5 minutes. Season with salt and stir occasionally. Pour 3 tablespoons of the reserved cooking liquor into the sauce and continue to simmer for 2 minutes. Stir in the prawns and continue to cook for a further 3 minutes until they go pink.

3 Meanwhile, cook the pasta in a large saucepan with plenty of boiling salted water until al dente. Drain and tip into the pan with the seafood sauce. Add the clams and mussels with the parsley and stir until heated through.

4 Sprinkle over the lemon zest and mix gently over a low heat for 20 seconds to allow the flavours to combine. Serve immediately with a little glass of chilled white wine.

Aragosta all'olio e limone

Lobster with lemon and extra virgin olive oil

If you're out to impress someone and have a passionate night – this is the recipe for you. Some foods put you in the mind for love either because of their appearance, because they are rich in certain minerals, or because they heat up our bodies, but lobster's claim to being a natural aphrodisiac is mainly down to its status as a symbol of luxury that dates right back to the Ancient Greeks. Today we know that lobster contains many nutrients is an ideal source of low-fat protein. It is also a source of zinc and B-12, both necessary nutrients for maintaining sexual desire – so enjoy your meal ... and the rest of your evening!

Serves 2

260 cals	18.3g fat	2.7g saturates	0.1g sugar	1.2g salt

1 large whole lobster, live

lemon

3 tablespoons extra virgin olive oil

Salt and freshly ground black pepper

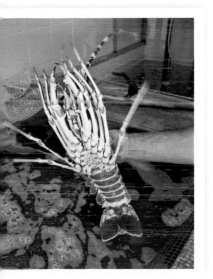

1 Bring a large pot of salted water to the boil a large pot. Plunge the live lobster into the boiling water and cook for 10 minutes exactly. Meanwhile, prepare a large bowl with very cold water. Add in a few ice cubes if necessary. Remove the lobster from the boiling water and drop immediately into the cold water for 2 minutes. Preheat the grill to the highest setting.

2 Place the lobster on a large chopping board and, holding it steady with one hand, cut from the top of the head straight down to the end of the tail using a cleaver or a large heavy knife. Use the same technique to cut the top half of the lobster. You should have now the lobster separated in two halves.

3 Twist the claws away from the body and use a large sharp knife to cut the shell. The best way to do this is by holding the knife in place with one hand and banging the top of it down with the other hand. Pick out the flesh and place on top of the two lobster halves. Now squeeze the lemon juice all over the flesh, drizzle over the oil and season with salt and pepper.

4 Place the two halves, flesh side up, under the hot grill for 1 minute. Please make sure that you don't overcook the lobster otherwise it will be chewy. Serve immediately accompanied with a fresh couscous salad.

Gamberoni al pomodoro
King prawns with olives and spicy tomato sauce

When I was growing up, prawns were often on the menu, either in salads or with pasta, but cooked this way has to be my favourite dish. I still recall how I always wanted more sauce so I could enjoy the prawns then soak up the rest with the warm crusty bread. I have put this in my Dinner for Two section, and you may wonder if it will fill you up as a main but I can assure you it does; in fact for a starter you would need only three prawns per person, not five.

Serves 2

318 cals	15.1g fat	2.2g saturates	6.9g sugar	2.8g salt

2 tablespoons olive oil

1 garlic clove, finely sliced

2 tablespoons kalamata olives, pitted and halved

½ teaspoon dried chilli flakes

1 tablespoon salted capers, rinsed under cold water

1 x 400g can chopped tomatoes

1 teaspoon dried oregano

10 uncooked king prawns, heads and shells on

4 thin slices of ciabatta bread, toasted, to serve

Salt and freshly ground black pepper

1 Place a large frying pan over a low heat, pour in the oil and cook the garlic for 30 seconds until soft and gold. Stir in the olives, chilli flakes and capers and continue to cook for a further 30 seconds. Pour in the chopped tomatoes with the oregano, season with salt and simmer gently, uncovered, for about 10 minutes, stirring occasionally.

2 Add the prawns into the sauce and continue to cook gently for a further 8 minutes. After 4 minutes turn over the prawns.

3 Once ready, place some of the tomato sauce in the middle of a serving plate and place 5 prawns on top. Try to cross the prawns together so they sit up on the plate. Serve immediately accompanied by the toasted ciabatta.

Tip

Who would have thought that you could get some exercise done while loading and unloading the dishwasher? When you reach for an item to unload, add a squat, slowly standing back up each time. It may take longer to load or unload the dishwasher but adding some basic squats can help tone.

Sogliola al forno con salsa verde
Baked sole with salsa verde

This is a fantastic dish for two as you literally share the plate and sit as close as you can to each other. The fish will be soft as butter and the salsa verde has a gorgeous fresh flavour. Please ensure you buy a large fish as instructed or the evening might end up in arguing over who gets the last mouthful. You can also make this with sea bass if you prefer.

Serves 2

593	cals	18.7g	fat	2.6g	saturates	1.6g	sugar	2.5g	salt

1 whole sole, about 1.2kg, skin, tail and head on

4 thin slices of toasted ciabatta bread, to serve

Salt and white pepper to taste

for the salsa verde

15 large basil leaves

3 tablespoons flat-leaf parsley

1 tablespoon freshly squeezed lemon juice

1 garlic clove, peeled

1 tablespoon salted capers, rinsed under cold water

3 tablespoons cold water

20ml extra virgin olive oil

1 Preheat the oven to 190°C/gas mark 5. Prepare the salsa verde by placing all the ingredients in a food processor and blitz for 30 seconds. Pour the salsa verde into a small bowl and set aside.

2 Score the flesh of the sole quite deeply on both sides at 5cm intervals. Season all over with salt and pepper and place the sole, pale skin-side down, in a large roasting tray. Pour in enough water to cover half the sole. Transfer the tray to the middle of the oven and bake for 35 minutes.

3 Remove the tray from the oven and gently lift the sole onto a large oval serving plate. Carefully remove the top skin using a fork.

4 Spoon over the salsa verde, serve with the toasted ciabatta and enjoy sharing it with your loved one.

Tip

Working out to stay in shape is fine, but setting a goal – such as finishing a 10k race or completing a rough water swim – will give your daily workouts more meaning.

Salmone in camicia
Salmon and leek parcels with smoked paprika

I often get asked how to make salmon a bit fancier, so here's how. The finished dish looks amazing, and the simple leek sauce and crispy pastry gives the fish a completely different dimension. The combination of flavours works beautifully and you'll be left feeling full and satisfied. You can also serve this as a starter – just make slightly smaller parcels (say about 60g each).

Serves 2

495 cals	29.3g fat	9.9g saturates	7.5g sugar	0.8g salt

1 large leek, trimmed and
  finely chopped

1 tablespoon olive oil

80g ricotta cheese

½ teaspoon smoked paprika

6 sheets filo pastry, 20 x 20cm

20g unsalted butter, melted

2 skinless salmon fillets, each
  about 100g

2 large round tomatoes,
  to serve

Salt

1 Put the chopped leek into a large frying pan with 2 tablespoons of water and the olive oil and cook over a medium heat for 10 minutes, stirring occasionally, until softened. Season with salt. Remove from the heat and tip the leeks into a large bowl. Set aside to cool. Mix in the ricotta cheese and the paprika. Preheat the oven to 200°C/gas mark 6.

2 To assemble the parcels, brush a sheet of filo pastry with melted butter, than lay 2 more sheets on top, brushing between each layer. Place a salmon fillet in the centre, season with a pinch of salt then spoon over half the leek mixture.

3 Fold the ends over the top; pull up the sides and scrunch together to enclose the contents. Repeat to make a second parcel, then brush both parcels with a little melted butter. Transfer the parcels to a lightly greased baking sheet and cook in the middle of the oven for 25 minutes until browned and crisp.

4 Slice the tomatoes into rounds about ½ cm thick. Overlap the slices in a circle on 2 serving plates, leaving a hole in the centre of the plate. Place the salmon parcels on top of the tomatoes and serve.

Pollo al pepe e limone
Glazed lemon pepper chicken

I have often used this marinade for chicken during the summer months when barbecuing, although I love it so much I've started to use it for roasting – it's just as good.

Serves 2

419	cals	13.3g	fat	2.2g	saturates	17.1g	sugar	0.7g	salt

2 medium skinless, boneless chicken breasts

2 tablespoons runny honey

Grated zest and juice of unwaxed lemon

1 garlic clove, peeled and crushed

1 teaspoon Dijon mustard

1 teaspoon freshly ground black pepper

300g baby salad potatoes, washed

2 tablespoons olive oil

Salt

1 Using a sharp knife, slash each chicken breast four times, cutting through to the middle of the breast. Mix the honey, lemon zest and juice, garlic, mustard and black pepper together in a medium bowl.

2 Add the chicken to the marinade and turn to coat evenly. Cover with clingfilm and place in the fridge to marinate for 1 hour. Preheat the oven to 220°C/gas mark 7.

3 Arrange the potatoes and chicken in a baking tray in a single layer. Pour over any remaining marinade and drizzle the oil on top. Season with salt and transfer the tray to the middle of the oven to cook for 30 minutes. Serve immediately with a little cavolo nero on the side.

Scaloppine al Martini e pepe rosa

Breast of chicken in Martini and pink peppercorn sauce

One of my favourite drinks is a Martini and vodka so I was tempted to try and come up with a recipe that uses them. This dish is quick and easy to prepare yet tastes as if you've marinated it all day. In fact, I have omitted the vodka from this particular recipe as I feel it is perfect with just the sweet Martini but by all means try it with 60ml Martini and 20ml vodka for a stronger flavour. You can also substitute veal for the chicken if you prefer.

Serves 2

495	cals	19.8g	fat	9g	saturates	13.7g	sugar	0.7g	salt

2 medium (each about 120g) skinless chicken breasts

3 tablespoons plain white flour

2 tablespoons salted butter

1 tablespoon olive oil

1 tablespoon pink peppercorns in brine, drained

80ml sweet Martini Bianco (do not be tempted to use the dry version)

Salt

1 Place the chicken breasts on a chopping board between 2 sheets of clingfilm. With the help of a kitchen mallet, gently bat out the meat until ½ cm thick. Sprinkle the flour on a flat plate and season with salt. Place the chicken breasts in the seasoned flour, turning to coat both sides, then slap the meat to remove any excess flour.

2 Melt half the butter with the oil in a large non-stick frying pan over a medium heat. Put the chicken in the pan and gently fry for 2 minutes. Add the peppercorns, turn the meat over and cook for 1 minute. Pour in the Martini and allow to flame. Cook for a further minute and season with salt.

3 Transfer the chicken to 2 warm serving plates. Add the remaining butter to the sauce. Stir over a low heat to mix well then pour the sauce over the chicken.

4 Serve immediately with a simple rocket salad dressed with extra virgin olive oil, a squeeze of fresh lemon juice and a pinch of sea salt.

Filetto di manzo al brandy
Fillet steaks with flambéd brandy sauce

I adore meat and really enjoy the natural flavours of a char-grilled steak but many like to serve steak, especially fillet, with a sauce. My wife absolutely loves me to bits when I make this for her, so all you guys out there, try cooking this easy recipe for your partner – you will be loved forever! It's just a little bit more special than a creamy peppercorn sauce as a kick from the alcohol adds to an already sublime combination. Try making this recipe with Marsala wine instead of brandy as that also works beautifully.

Serves 2

499 cals	31.5g fat	15.2g saturates	0.5g sugar	1.4g salt

2 fillet steaks, about 180g each

2 teaspoons coarsely ground black pepper

1 tablespoon olive oil

2 knobs butter

3 tablespoons brandy

2 tablespoons white wine

50ml beef stock

1 tablespoon green peppercorns in brine, drained

40ml double cream

Salt to taste

1 Rub the steaks all over with the coarsely ground black pepper. Heat the oil with 1 knob of butter in a medium frying pan. Immediately the butter stops foaming, add in the steaks. Cook for 4 minutes on each side for medium cooked steak. Transfer the meat to a warm plate, season with salt and set aside in a warm place to rest for 3–4 minutes.

2 Tip away the excess fat from the pan; pour in the brandy and flambé to burn off the alcohol, stirring with a wooden spoon to scrape the meat juices from the base of the pan. Pour in the wine and cook until it has reduced by half. Add in the stock and continue to cook over a high heat until the sauce is well reduced, stirring occasionally.

3 Stir in the peppercorns with the cream and the remaining butter and cook for a further 2 minutes, stirring continuously.

4 Place each steak in the middle of a warm serving plate and pour over the sauce. Serve immediately with a little salad of your choice.

Gelato cotto in meringa
Baked ice cream in crispy meringue

Now, I admit that the calories for this are a little high, but I wanted to include it as it's the perfect way to end a special dinner for two – just don't eat it too often! You could always encourage your partner to join you in a workout to help burn off the extra calories. It needs to be prepared there and then but your partner will be extremely impressed watching you make it and the final outcome is amazing. Make sure the ice cream has just come out of the freezer and that you completely cover the sponge with the meringue.

Serves 2

643 cals	25.6g fat	4.8g saturates	82.1g sugar	0.7g salt

2 x 35g mini cake sponges
1 tablespoon brandy
2 tablespoons raspberry jam
3 egg whites
4 tablespoons caster sugar
40g hazelnuts, finely chopped
2 balls low-fat vanilla ice cream
150g fresh raspberries

1 Place each sponge in the middle of the serving plates and drizzle over the brandy. Carefully spread the jam on top. In a large clean mixing bowl, whisk the egg whites until stiff. Slowly add in the sugar a little at time to create a glossy meringue. Gently fold in the hazelnuts.

2 Place one ice cream ball in the middle of each sponge. Arrange some raspberries on top of the sponge all around the ice cream. Spoon the meringue over the ice cream and raspberries, ensuring that the sponge and ice cream are completely covered.

3 Using a blow torch, flame all around the meringue mixture until it is tinged with golden. Serve immediately.

One pot meals

Zuppa di verdure all'ortolana
Chunky winter vegetable and cannellini bean soup

I created this soup when I was cooking for friends who are vegetarian and they all watched me and wrote down the recipe so I figured if they were impressed, hopefully you will be too. I have used six different kinds of vegetables to make the wholesome soup you'd expect but the bread, cheese and beans give it an even more rustic feel. It's the perfect evening family meal or a great starter for friends (do ensure you serve small portions as a starter as it's extremely filling).

Serves 6

| 335 cals | 12g fat | 5g saturates | 10.3g sugar | 5.8g salt |

2 tablespoons extra virgin olive oil

1 red onion, roughly chopped

2 carrots, peeled and roughly chopped

2 turnips, roughly chopped

2 celery stalks, washed and roughly chopped

150g curly Savoy cabbage, trimmed and roughly chopped

1 bay leaf

1.5 litres warm vegetable stock

1 x 400g can cannellini beans, drained

150g (prepared weight) pumpkin, cut into 2cm cubes

4 tablespoons chopped flat-leaf parsley

6 slices of rustic country-style bread

1 garlic clove, halved

100g freshly grated Pecorino cheese

Salt and white pepper to taste

1 Heat the olive oil in a large saucepan and fry the onion, carrots, turnips, celery, cabbage and bay leaf for 5 minutes until golden, stirring occasionally with a wooden spoon. Pour in the vegetable stock and gently simmer for 20 minutes, stirring occasionally, until all the vegetables are soft.

2 Add the beans and the pumpkin, season and continue to cook for a further 15 minutes. Stir in the parsley and allow to rest for 3 minutes. Preheat a griddle pan.

3 Toast the bread on the griddle pan for about 2 minutes on each side until golden and crispy. Immediately lightly rub with the garlic on one side only.

4 To serve, place a slice of bread in 6 warm serving bowls and pour over the soup. Sprinkle with Pecorino and serve immediately.

Zuppa di piselli e pesto
Fresh pea and basil pesto soup

Serves 4

228 cals	16.3g fat	7.8g saturates	3.7g sugar	1g salt

1 tablespoon salted butter

4 shallots, finely chopped

400g fresh peas, podded weight

500ml water

1 vegetable stock cube

2 tablespoons ready-made basil pesto

60ml double cream plus a little extra to garnish

Salt and freshly ground white pepper

1 Melt the butter in a large saucepan over a medium heat and cook the shallots for 5 minutes, stirring occasionally with a wooden spoon. Add in the peas with the water and the stock cube and bring to the boil.

2 Lower the heat, add in the pesto and cover the pan. Simmer for about 15 minutes. Stir occasionally.

3 When the peas are tender, ladle them into a food processor or blender with a little of the cooking liquid. Blitz until smooth.

4 Return the soup to the pan, pour in half of the cream, season and reheat. Serve in warmed bowls, garnished with cream.

Zuppa di cipolle
Onion and bacon soup

Serves 4

266 cals	16g fat	3.3g saturates	14.2g sugar	3.4g salt

150g pancetta or bacon rashers, rinds removed and cut into 1cm pieces

4 tablespoons extra virgin olive oil

800g white onions, peeled and finely sliced

1.5 litres warm vegetable stock

1 x 400g can chopped tomatoes

2 tablespoons freshly chopped flat-leaf parsley

4 tablespoons freshly grated Grana Padano cheese

Salt and freshly ground white pepper

1 Put the pancetta in a large saucepan over a medium heat and allow to sizzle for 2 minutes, stirring constantly with a wooden spoon. Pour in the oil then add the onions and stir everything together. Lower the heat and cook for 25 minutes, stirring occasionally, until the onions take on a beautiful golden colour.

2 Once the onions are coloured, pour in the stock and the chopped tomatoes. Season and bring to the boil. Lower the heat, half cover the pan with the lid and simmer for 35 minutes, stirring occasionally. After 30 minutes, check the consistency of the soup and add a little more stock or water if it is too thick.

3 Stir in the parsley and check the seasoning. Serve in 4 warmed bowls, topped with a sprinkling of Grana Padano.

Pasta e fagioli classica
Neapolitan pasta with three-bean sauce

In the village I come from, many people are quite poor and eat meat sparingly. They often cook with beans, which give you all the goodness your body needs and leave you feeling extremely full. This is a very rustic traditional recipe that every nonna (grandmother) knows how to cook.

Serves 4

506 cals	17g fat	4.1g saturates	6.1g sugar	2.7g salt

2 tablespoons olive oil

1 large onion, peeled and finely chopped

100g diced pancetta

2 tablespoons chopped fresh rosemary leaves

1 x 400g can borlotti beans, drained

1 x 400g can cannellini beans, drained

1 x 400g can chick peas, drained

2 chicken stock cubes

200g dried pasta shells

Salt and freshly ground black pepper

1 Pour the oil into a large saucepan over a medium heat and cook the onion and pancetta for 5 minutes, stirring occasionally with a wooden spoon. Add the rosemary and continue to cook for 2 minutes. Tip in all the beans, stir gently together and cook for a further 2 minutes.

2 Add the stock cubes with 1.7 litres of boiling water. Stir and leave to simmer over a low heat for 15 minutes, stirring every 5 minutes. Add the pasta to the same pan and continue to cook over a low heat. (If the sauce becomes too thick, stir in a glassful of hot water from the kettle.)

3 Cook until the pasta is al dente, then turn off the heat and leave to rest for 2 minutes before serving. Divide the pasta between 4 serving bowls and enjoy with a cold Italian beer.

Conchigliette e cavolfiori
Shell pasta with cauliflower, pancetta and parmesan

Is it a soup? Is it a pasta dish? It's a combination of the two, and everyone I've made it for absolutely loves it. It's comfort food that you can eat on the sofa watching a movie, bowl in one hand and spoon in another, loving every mouthful and feeling that you are truly being looked after. It's one of those dishes that just makes you feel good. It is definitely an all-year round meal but somehow tastes so much better with the rain beating down (so no problem in Britain, we're lucky here I guess, since it seems to rain more often than not!)

Serves 4

468 cals	26.7g fat	8.1g saturates	6.7g sugar	3.3g salt

3 tablespoons olive oil

1 large white onion, peeled and finely chopped

100g diced pancetta

300g cauliflower florets, quartered

1.8 litres hot chicken stock, made with 3 chicken stock cubes

150g conchigliette (small shell pasta)

3 medium eggs

50g freshly grated Parmesan cheese

2 tablespoons chopped flat-leaf parsley

Salt and freshly ground white pepper

1 Heat the olive oil in a large saucepan and fry the onion over a medium heat for 3 minutes until golden. Add the pancetta and continue to fry for 5 minutes. Stir occasionally with a wooden spoon. Add in the cauliflower and fry everything together for a further 2 minutes, stirring occasionally with a wooden spoon.

2 Pour in the stock, lower the heat and leave to simmer for 20 minutes with the lid half on. Stir occasionally.

3 Remove the lid and season with salt and pepper. Tip in the pasta, lower the heat and cook the pasta in the cauliflower broth for about 7 minutes until al dente. Stir gently every 2 minutes.

4 Remove the pan from the heat. Crack in the eggs and mix everything together for 30 seconds, allowing the broth to thicken and the eggs to scramble into the sauce. Stir in the Parmesan and parsley, and serve.

Risotto allo zafferano e pollo
Simple chicken and saffron risotto

Many people tell me they're frightened to make risottos, yet they are so incredibly easy. You just need to make sure you have half an hour to stay by the hob as the risotto will need constant stirring, and ensure all your ingredients are prepared when you start. It can't get simpler than that.

Serves 6

565	cals	23.3g	fat	9.3g	saturates	1.8g	sugar	1.9g	salt

Pinch of good-quality saffron

1.5 litres hot chicken stock, made with stock cubes

5 tablespoons olive oil

1 red onion, peeled and finely chopped

400g arborio or carnaroli rice

150ml white wine

3 medium skinless, boneless chicken breasts, cut into 2cm pieces

60g salted butter

80g Parmesan cheese

Salt and freshly ground black pepper

1 Mix the saffron with 4 tablespoons of hot stock in a small bowl. Set aside. Heat the oil in a large, heavy-based saucepan and fry the onion, stirring with a wooden spoon, until soft but not browned. Tip in the rice and fry for 3 minutes over a medium heat, stirring continuously, to allow the rice to toast in the hot oil. Pour the wine over the rice and continue to cook for a further minute to evaporate the alcohol.

2 Add the chicken pieces and pour over the reserved saffron, along with a couple of ladlefuls of stock and bring to a simmer. Continue to cook and stir until all the stock is absorbed. At this point please stay with the saucepan because I need you to keep stirring with a wooden spoon.

3 Continue to add stock, a little at the time, stirring all the while, and allow the rice to absorb each addition before adding any more. This will take between 20 and 22 minutes; you may not need to add all the stock.

4 Once the rice is cooked, remove the pan from the heat and add the butter with the Parmesan. Stir everything together for 30 seconds, allowing the risotto to become creamy. Season with salt and pepper and serve immediately.

Risotto ai funghi e piselli
Mushrooms and peas risotto

OK, you have guests coming over for dinner and it seemed like a really good idea at the time, but now the day has arrived, you just don't have time to spend hours in the kitchen – this is the recipe for you. It will guarantee complete enjoyment all around but will take minutes to prepare.

Serves 4

492	cals	17.6g	fat	5.9g	saturates	4.8g	sugar	1.7g	salt

20g sliced dried Porcini mushrooms

3 tablespoons olive oil

1 large onion, finely chopped

2 tablespoons fresh rosemary leaves, finely chopped

150g chestnut mushrooms, sliced

300g Arborio or Carnaroli rice

150g frozen peas, defrosted

1.2 litres warm vegetable stock, made with 2 stock cubes

30g salted butter

40g freshly grated Parmesan cheese

Salt and white pepper

1 In a medium size bowl, cover the dried Porcini mushrooms with cold water and soak for 30 minutes. Once softened, drain and reserve the flavoured water. Meanwhile, heat the oil in a large saucepan and fry the onion with the rosemary over a medium heat for about 3 minutes. Stir occasionally with a wooden spoon. Add in all the mushrooms and continue to cook for a further 3 minutes stirring occasionally.

2 Pour in the rice and stir continuously for 2 minutes allowing the grains to toast in the olive oil and begin to absorb all the mushroom flavours. Pour in the water from the soaked Porcini mushrooms and continue to cook for a further minute.

3 Add in the peas and start to pour the warm stock a little at a time, stirring occasionally, allowing the rice to absorb the stock before adding more. Season with salt and pepper and cook gently on a low heat. If you need extra liquid, use warm water.

4 After about 18 minutes, when most of the stock has been absorbed, remove the saucepan from the heat and stir the butter into the risotto. It is very important that you stir the butter very fast into the rice for at least 15 seconds – this will create a fantastic creamy texture. Finally, stir in the Parmesan cheese and serve immediately.

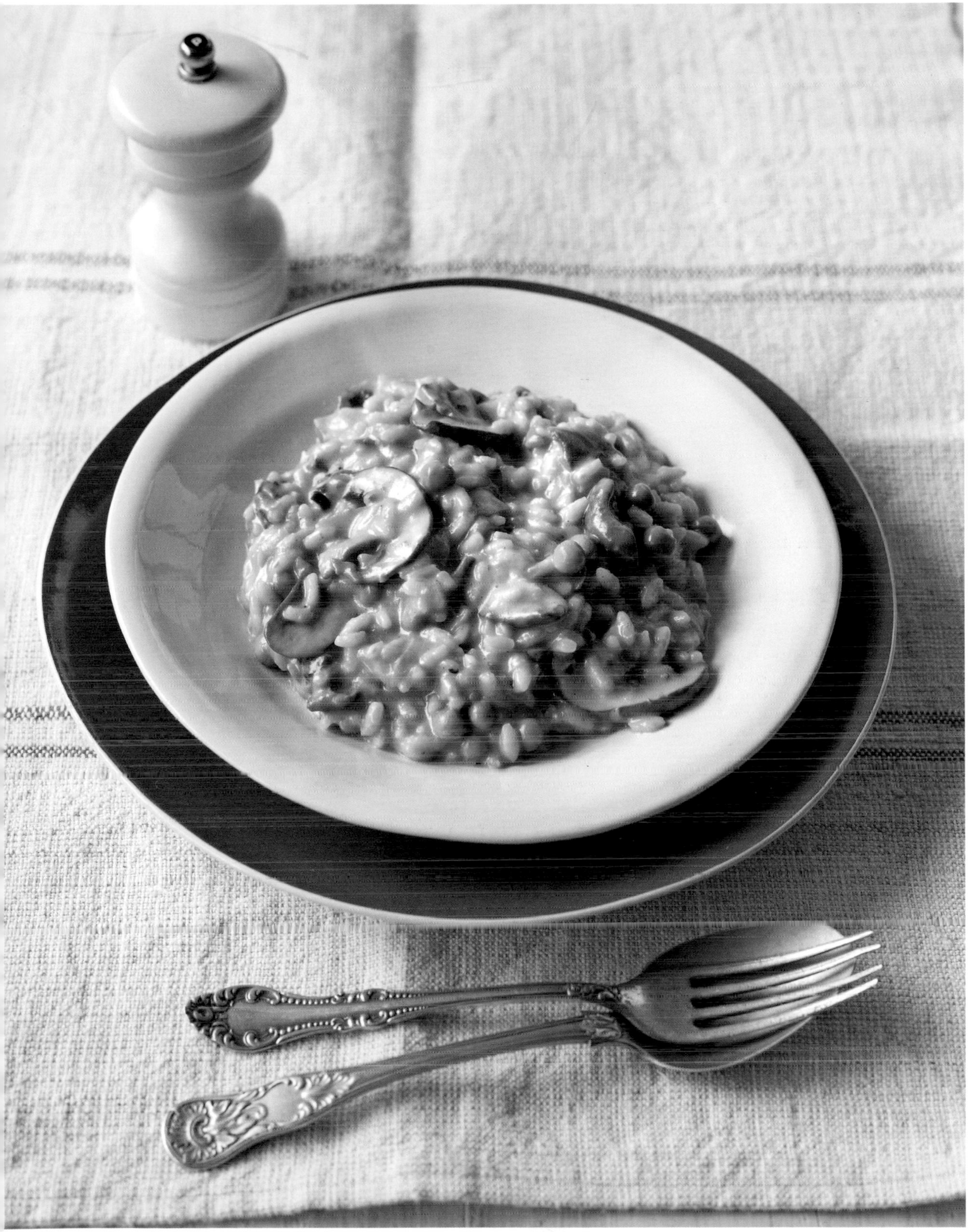

Risotto con carciofi e zucca
Artichoke, butternut squash and white wine risotto

Once you have mastered a basic risotto, you can let your creative curiousity run wild. Pretty much anything goes, but I created this one because I love artichokes and find that we tend not to use them enough. Squash and artichokes are both incredibly healthy. Did you know that artichokes are one of the healthiest foods in the world? They are high in fibre, helping to reduce cholesterol reduction and aid better digestion and increased bile flow; they are high in antioxidants, believed to help prevent cancer and are good for the liver – why don't we eat more of them? They have to be in the running for top veg the year!

Serves 4

510	cals	22.3g	fat	5.5g	saturates	5.6g	sugar	2g	salt

3 tablespoons extra virgin olive oil

1 red onion, peeled and finely chopped

250g arborio or carnaroli rice

2 tablespoons fresh rosemary leaves, finely chopped

150ml white wine

250g butternut squash, peeled and cut into 1cm cubes

10 chargrilled artichokes in oil, drained and quartered

800ml warm vegetable stock

1 teaspoon butter

60g freshly grated Parmesan cheese

Salt and freshly ground black pepper

1 Heat the oil in a large heavy-based saucepan and fry the onions, stirring with a wooden spoon, until soft but not browned. Tip in the rice with the rosemary and fry for 3 minutes over a medium heat, stirring continuously, to allow the rice to toast in the hot oil. Pour the wine over the rice and continue to cook for a further minute to evaporate the alcohol.

2 Add the squash and half the artichokes, along with a couple of ladlefuls of stock and bring to a simmer. Continue to cook and stir until all the stock is absorbed. At this point please stay with the saucepan because I need you to keep stirring with a wooden spoon.

3 Continue to add stock, a little at the time, stirring all the while, and allow the rice to absorb each addition before adding any more. Once the rice has begun to swell add the rest of the artichokes. Keep stirring and adding stock – this will take between 20 and 22 minutes; you may not need to add all the stock.

4 Once the squash is soft and the rice cooked, remove the pan from the heat and add the butter with the Parmesan. Stir everything together for 30 seconds, allowing the risotto to become creamy. Season with salt and pepper and serve immediately.

Pollo alla cacciatore
Hunter's-style chicken with pancetta and tomatoes

Lots of people favour chicken breasts, wings or legs but many underestimate the thighs, so here is a recipe that will change your mind about it. The thigh meat is really tender and cooked this way, remains as soft as butter. I've called this hunter's-style chicken as it reminds me of my grandfather Giovanni, who would use every bit of the chicken, but in different ways. He used to say: if you hunt for meat, don't waste any of it, create a way of enjoying your hard work – how I wish I could ask him how he hunted for chickens when he kept them in his back garden!

Serves 4

330 cals	16.9g fat	4.7g saturates	7.1g sugar	1.5g salt

2 tablespoons olive oil

100g cubed pancetta

2 red onions, peeled and finely sliced

1 tablespoon fresh, chopped rosemary leaves

500g skinless chicken thighs, each cut into 4 pieces

80ml white wine

1 x 400g can chopped tomatoes

2 bay leaves

Salt and freshly ground black pepper

1 Pour the oil into a heavy-based saucepan and fry the pancetta with the onions over a medium heat for 3 minutes, stirring occasionally with a wooden spoon. Add the rosemary and continue to cook for 1 minute. Add the chicken pieces, season and continue to cook for a further 2 minutes.

2 Pour in the wine and let it come to a bubble before adding the chopped tomatoes and bay leaves. Cover with the lid and allow the chicken to gently simmer for 15 minutes, stirring occasionally. Remove the lid and continue to cook for a further 5 minutes.

3 Allow the dish to rest off the heat for 3 minutes before serving with a little glass of cold Italian white wine.

Tip

Even the most out of shape cook can benefit from adding some countertop push ups to their daily routine. Position yourself about two feet from the countertop, with feet together. Extend your arms until they touch the edge of the kitchen countertop and slowly lean in. Once your chin is just above the countertop, use your arms to lift back up and repeat.

Ossobuco alla Milanese
Veal shanks with pancetta and white wine

PLEASE PLEASE, if you don't try all the recipes in this book, do try this one. Ossobuco is a traditional favourite in Italy, originally from the farming areas near Milan. The dish takes a little time to prepare but is truly worth it and you can cook it and then reheat and serve it that night or even the following day; in fact the flavours are better if you can make it in advance. Remember to suck on the bone once you've eaten all the meat, the marrow is amazing!

Serves 6

| 469 | cals | 21.5g | fat | 5.7g | saturates | 5g | sugar | 2.9g | salt |

5 tablespoons olive oil

100g diced pancetta

Plain white flour, for dusting

1.5kg veal shanks, 6 pieces about 7cm thick

1 onion, peeled and finely chopped

2 large celery stalks, finely chopped

2 carrots, peeled and finely chopped

3 garlic cloves, peeled and crushed

3 fresh thyme sprigs, plus extra to garnish

2 tablespoons tomato purée

100ml white wine

600ml warm chicken stock

Salt and freshly ground white pepper

1 Preheat the oven to 170°C/gas mark 3. Heat the oil in a large frying pan and fry the pancetta for 8 minutes until golden and crispy, stirring occasionally with a wooden spoon. Remove the pancetta from the pan using a slotted spoon and set aside on a plate lined with kitchen paper to absorb any excess oil.

2 Put the flour on a plate and season generously with salt and pepper. Coat the veal shanks in the flour then shake off the excess. Place the shanks in the same frying pan used to cook the pancetta. Fry the meat for 5 minutes on each side until sealed and browned all over. Remove the shanks from the pan and set aside on a plate.

3 Add the onion, celery, carrots and garlic to the frying pan and cook, stirring continuously, for 10 minutes until softened and beginning to brown. Add the thyme, cooked pancetta and the tomato purée and mix together. Pour in the white wine and simmer for 5 minutes to evaporate the alcohol. Pour in the stock and stir for a further 5 minutes.

4 Spoon a third of the vegetable sauce into a large casserole dish. Place the veal shanks on top. Pour over the remaining sauce, covering the meat as much as possible. Cover the dish with its lid and place in the oven for 1 hour. Remove the lid and continue to cook for a further 30 minutes. Serve immediately, garnished with fresh thyme sprigs, with a crispy salad of your choice.

Stufato di agnello e piselli
Lamb, pea and onion stew

If you're preparing a family meal or a meal for close friends, I really recommend this recipe. I love the fact that you can serve it on from the pot, hand everyone a fork and tuck in together. Of course, you can serve it for a dinner party, plated individually with rice, couscous or salad but there is something especially nice about sharing from the pot, and it makes the evening a far more relaxed experience. *Buonissimo!*

Serves 4

| 408 cals | 21.4g fat | 6.5g saturates | 6.4g sugar | 1g salt |

3 tablespoons olive oil

2 red onions, peeled and finely chopped

700g boneless stewing lamb, cut into 3cm cubes

140ml white wine

300g fresh or frozen peas (defrosted if using frozen ones)

2 tablespoons thyme leaves

250ml warm vegetable stock

Salt and freshly ground black pepper

1 Pour the oil into a large, heavy-based casserole and fry the onions over a medium heat for 3 minutes, stirring occasionally with a wooden spoon. Add the lamb cubes and continue to cook, turning the pieces, for about 10 minutes until the meat is brown on all sides. Pour in the wine and allow it to bubble for 2 minutes. Add the peas with the thyme, pour in the stock and bring to the boil.

2 Cover the dish with the lid and simmer gently for 1 hour, stirring occasionally with a wooden spoon. Remove the lid and continue to simmer for a further 30 minutes until the lamb is tender and the sauce has reduced.

3 Allow the dish to rest off the heat for 3 minutes then place in the centre of the table so that your family and friends can tuck in and enjoy the experience.

Did you know?

Italians love olive oil. They eat around 5tbsp a day. It's good news as olive oil is packed with monounsaturated fat – the type that helps to lower bad or LDL cholesterol and maintains good or HDL cholesterol. It's still high in calories though – each tablespoon contains 100 calories – so you do need to use it in moderation.

Agnello al forno alla Pugliese
Baked lamb with potatoes and pecorino cheese

I remember having this amazing meal around Easter time, which used to be a huge celebration in Italy. My mother would prepare this meal and leave it to cook while we all joined in games and activities in the streets. I remember walking home starving and smelling this amazing dish the minute we got into the house. The meat is as soft as butter and the potatoes crispy on top but soft through the layers. Lamb should definitely be used in season so if you fancy this during the winter months, try making it with neck of lamb or cubed beef.

Serves 6

346 cals   16.7g fat   3g saturates   2.6g sugar   1g salt

4 tablespoons extra virgin olive oil

800g floury potatoes, such as Maris Piper, peeled and cut into ½ cm thick slices

1.3kg boneless leg of lamb, trimmed and cut into 4cm cubes

500g cherry tomatoes, halved

2 tablespoons chopped fresh rosemary leaves

4 garlic cloves, peeled and chopped

100g Pecorino cheese

Salt and freshly ground black pepper

1 Preheat the oven to 180°C/gas mark 4. Pour half the oil into a lidded casserole dish measuring about 24cm in diameter with sides 10cm deep. Spread one-third of the potato slices over the base. Season with salt and pepper, scatter over half the meat cubes and season once more.

2 Squeeze the halved tomatoes over the sink to get rid of the seeds then scatter half of them over the lamb, along with half the rosemary and half the garlic. Season, then sprinkle over half the cheese.

3 Layer in another third of the potatoes, the remaining meat cubes and some seasoning, followed by the rest of the tomatoes, rosemary, garlic and a little more seasoning. Cover with the last of the potatoes, season for a final time and sprinkle over the remaining cheese and olive oil.

4 Cover with the lid and transfer to the oven to bake for 35 minutes. Uncover and continue to bake for a further 1 hour until the top is golden and crusty. Allow the dish to rest out of the oven for 10 minutes before serving.

A carn cu sugu
Neapolitan-style meat stew

This dish is for all you meat-lovers out there. It's quick and easy to prepare, provides a hugely fulfilling meal with bundles of flavours – and leaves no washing up. The recipe is all about the meat; the tomatoes and herbs just add in a touch more flavour while ensuring the meats remain extremely moist. It really is the perfect wholesome main course. Dipping bread into the sauce at the end is a must! You can also serve this stew with rice if you prefer.

Serves 4

607	cals	30.1g	fat	10g	saturates	15.1g	sugar	3g	salt

1 tablespoon extra virgin olive oil

1 medium onion, finely chopped

2 tablespoons fresh rosemary leaves

350g topside of beef, cut into 2cm chunks

8 small pork ribs

4 medium Italian-style pork sausages

3 x 400g cans chopped tomatoes

2 tablespoons tomato purée

5 basil leaves

Salt and freshly ground black pepper

8 thin slices of toasted ciabatta bread, to serve

1 Heat the oil in a large saucepan and cook the onion with the rosemary for 5 minutes until softened, stirring occasionally with a wooden spoon. Add in the beef, ribs and sausages and continue to cook over a medium heat for 5 minutes. Ensure that all the meat is sealed on all sides.

2 Stir in the chopped tomatoes, tomato purée, 100ml of hot water and the basil. Bring to the boil then lower the heat to a simmer. Season with salt and pepper, cover with a lid and leave to cook very gently for 2 hours until the sauce is thick and shiny. Please ensure that you stir the sauce every 20 minutes and if necessary add a little more hot water if the dish needs more liquid.

3 Serve hot in nice rustic bowls accompanied with toasted bread.

Calamari all' arrabbiata
Slow-cooked squid in spicy tomato sauce

Living in England, I have learned that many people only associate squid with eating it fried in batter but there is so much more you can do with this delicacy and I hope you'll try this and love it as much as I do. If you prefer, ask your fishmonger to prepare the squid for you (even though for me that's the best part) and ensure you don't over-cook it, as it will become too hard and chewy. Enjoy the chilli kick!

Serves 4

| 330 | cals | 20.3g | fat | 3.1g | saturates | 3.2g | sugar | 0.7g | salt |

600g fresh squid

100ml olive oil

3 garlic cloves, peeled and crushed

1 teaspoon dried chilli flakes

200ml dry white wine

1 x 400g can chopped tomatoes

2 tablespoons chopped flat-leaf parsley

Salt

1 To prepare the squid, first pull away the tentacles from the body and then remove the quill. (It looks like a long piece of clear plastic.) Next pull the wings away from the body, peel off the grey membrane and set aside. Peel away the thin purple membrane from the body of the squid. Turn the squid inside out and wash under cold running water. Set aside.

2 Cut the tentacles away from the head, just behind the eyes. Pull out the hard beak and discard. Slice the body of the squid into 1cm rings and the wings into 1cm thick slices.

3 Gently heat the oil in a large frying pan and fry the garlic and chilli for 30 seconds. Add the squid and let it cook for 8 minutes so that the water is released. Stir occasionally with a wooden spoon. Pour in the wine and continue to cook for a further 2 minutes. Add the chopped tomatoes into the frying pan and bring to the boil.

4 Lower the heat, mix in the parsley and simmer, uncovered, for 1 hour. Stir with a wooden spoon every 10 minutes. Season with salt and serve hot with warm crusty bread.

Entertaining

Popcorn piccanti
Spicy party popcorn

Often you would hand round nuts or crisps with drinks before a dinner party, but hardly anyone thinks to serve popcorn. It delivers the same salty taste that people love to nibble on, yet it's lot lighter and healthier. It seems to put guests in a great mood too, perhaps because popcorn brings back nice memories of childhood trips to the cinema. Trust me – you'll need to make double quantities!

Serves 6

186 cals	**7.2g** fat	**3.2g** saturates	**1.1g** sugar	**1.7g** salt

1 tablespoon olive oil
250g popping corn
30g unsalted butter
1 teaspoon chilli powder
1 teaspoon smoked paprika
1 teaspoon ground cumin
1 teaspoon caster sugar
2 teaspoons table salt

1 Pour the oil into a large lidded saucepan and place over a high heat. Tip in the popcorn and quickly cover with the lid. Leave the popcorn to pop, giving the pan a shake every now and then to keep the kernels moving. Once all the kernels are popped (the knocking sound will stop), remove the pan from the heat and set aside.

2 Melt the butter in a small saucepan with the remaining ingredients and mix everything together for 15 seconds. Pour the spicy butter over the popcorn and transfer everything to a large clean paper carrier bag.

3 Holding the top of the bag tightly closed, shake the bag to ensure all the popcorn is beautifully coated with the spicy butter. Tip the popcorn into party bowls and serve warm.

Tip
A handful of roasted peanuts equals 155 calories. Skip for 14 minutes to compensate.

Asparagi con cipolline e pancetta
Asparagus and spring onions wrapped in pancetta

I have my boys, Luciano and Rocco, to thank for this recipe. They both love asparagus and wrapping the spears in pancetta made it even tastier and more exciting for them. Cooking spring onions in the same way gives the dish an even more sophisticated flavour and it works beautifully when you're entertaining, either served as tasty light nibbles or as a side dish to a main. Please try this when asparagus in season – the flavour really is so much better. You can use Parma ham instead of pancetta if you prefer.

Serves 6

253	cals	22.9g	fat	9.8g	saturates	2.2g	sugar	1.6g	salt

600g asparagus spears

Handful of spring onions

12 slices of pancetta or streaky bacon, fat removed

60g salted butter

2 tablespoons olive oil

Salt and freshly ground black pepper

1 Snap off the woody stems from the asparagus and trim away the roots from the spring onions. Bring a medium saucepan of salted water to the boil, drop in the asparagus and cook for 4 minutes. Add the spring onions and continue to cook for a further 4 minutes. Prepare a large bowl with very cold water. (Add a few ice cubes if necessary.)

2 Drain the asparagus and spring onions and immediately immerse them in the cold water for 5 minutes. By using this method, the asparagus and spring onions will not lose their bright green colour.

3 Drain the vegetables again, place on a chopping board and arrange into six even bunches. Wrap the middle of each bunch with 2 slices of pancetta to secure.

4 Heat the butter and oil in a large frying pan, add in the asparagus bundles and fry gently until the pancetta becomes golden and crispy. Season with salt and pepper and serve hot with a spoonful of the buttery oil poured over the top.

Zuppa di pomodori e basilico
Traditional tomato and basil soup

Soups make fabulous starters and you can create some amazing different flavours but we've all forgotten about traditional tomato soup, which has to be one of the lightest options anyone could come up with. I was on holiday and my family were served a small glass of tomato soup as an aperitif. My son Rocco was amazed by it and thought he'd never tasted anything so great. That small glass confirmed for me once again that going back to basics and keeping it simple with a few ingredients will always work. Rocco this recipe is dedicated to you – as you say – keeping it real!

Serves 8

| 112 | cals | **6.7g** | fat | **1.2g** | saturates | **7.7g** | sugar | **2.3g** | salt |

3 tablespoons olive oil

1 red onion, finely chopped

1 celery stalk, halved

1 carrot, peeled and halved lengthways

2 garlic cloves, peeled and squashed

1kg ripe plum tomatoes, quartered

1 teaspoon fresh oregano leaves

20 basil leaves, reserving 8 for garnish

2 tablespoons tomato purée

1 litre vegetable stock, made with stock cubes

150g sun-dried tomatoes in oil, drained

Salt and freshly ground black pepper

1 Heat the oil in a large heavy-based saucepan and fry the onion, celery, carrot and garlic for 2 minutes over a medium heat. Season with salt and pepper and stir occasionally using a wooden spoon. Add the tomatoes, herbs and tomato purée and continue to fry for a further 10 minutes, stirring occasionally. Pour in the stock and bring it to the boil. Simmer, uncovered, for 25 minutes.

2 Remove the saucepan from the heat and discard the garlic, carrot and celery. Stir in the sun-dried tomatoes. Using a stick blender, blitz the soup to a smooth purée.

3 Return the soup to a low heat for 2 minutes and check the seasoning. Serve hot in warm bowls, garnished with a single basil leaf on top.

Carpaccio di salmone
Fresh salmon carpaccio with chilli and oregano

Raw meat and fish is really in fashion at the moment but more importantly, it's really good for you. If ever you have dinner guests whom you don't know that well, this is a really safe dish that everyone will enjoy. It's extremely light and yet still full of flavour. If you prefer, ask your fishmonger to skin the fish for you and you could substitute the salmon with tuna if you fancy a meatier texture.

Serves 4

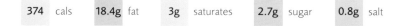

| 374 cals | 18.4g fat | 3g saturates | 2.7g sugar | 0.8g salt |

700g salmon fillet, skin on

15 cherry tomatoes, halved

5 tablespoons freshly squeezed lemon juice

2 tablespoons extra virgin olive oil

½ teaspoon dry chilli flakes

3 tablespoons fresh oregano leaves

12 thin slices of ciabatta bread, toasted, to serve

Salt

1 Place the salmon on a chopping board, skin-side down. Using a very sharp long-bladed knife, cut as finely as you can along the length of the fillet. Discard the skin. Place the salmon slices, side by side, on a large cold serving plate.

2 Using your fingertips, squeeze the juice and the pulp from the halved tomatoes all over the salmon. Scatter the skins on top of the fish. Drizzle over the lemon juice and oil. Season with salt and sprinkle over the chilli flakes and oregano leaves.

3 Cover with clingfilm and chill in the fridge for about 20 minutes until the fish is opaque. Serve as a starter with a few slices of toasted ciabatta.

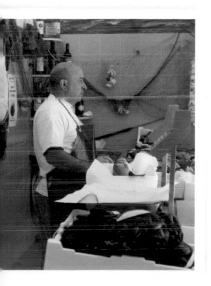

Spigola al forno in crosta di sale
Baked seabass in a thyme-flavoured salt crust

Italy has thousands of miles of coastline, lakes and rivers, so we have a lot of recipes for fish. One very traditional way of cooking a whole fish is to bake it in salt. The thick coating dries to form a case and ensures the fish inside stays moist and full of flavour. There is something really impressive about serving a whole fish – it has a real wow factor. Your guests will feel very special and yet baking in salt is so easy. You can cook any whole fish this way – try it with sardines if you prefer.

Serves 4

| 382 cals | 28.9g fat | 4.2g saturates | 0.6g sugar | 2.5g salt |

1kg whole seabass, gutted, but with head, tail and skin on

1.2kg rock salt

4 tablespoons thyme leaves

Cold water as necessary

100g crispy mixed salad leaves

for the dressing

100ml extra virgin olive oil

Juice of 1 large size lemon

2 tablespoons chopped flat-leaf parsley

Salt and freshly ground black pepper

1 Preheat the oven to 200°/gas mark 6. Wash and clean the gutted fish under cold running water, but do not remove the scales. Tip in enough salt to form a 1cm-thick layer over the base of a baking tray large enough to contain the seabass.

2 Pour the rest of the salt into a large bowl with the thyme. Mix in enough water to moisten but not over-wet the salt: you want a stiff slush that can be patted into shape. Place the fish on the layer of salt on the baking tray and cover with the remaining thyme-flavoured salt. The fish should be completely encased. Transfer the tray to the middle of the oven and bake for 25 minutes.

3 Meanwhile, pour the oil and lemon in a small bowl and sprinkle over the parsley. Season with salt and pepper and whisk everything together to create a dressing. Set aside.

4 To serve, crack open the salt crust using a spoon and lift off any large pieces of salt. Use a pastry brush to push away any remaining pieces. Cut the skin on either side of the seabass by pulling it away with a fork. Lift up the skin, remove and discard.

5 Run the tip of the fork down the centre of the fish, just to one side of the spine. Gently lift the first fillet onto a warm serving plate. Do the same on the other side. Turn the fish over and repeat the process.

6 Once all four fillets are on the serving plate, drizzle over three-quarters of the prepared dressing. Serve immediately with a little crispy salad tossed with the remaining lemon dressing.

Merluzzo piccante
Baked fillet of cod in spicy red salsa

Many people who don't like fish nonetheless love this recipe because cod is not strongly flavoured and the red salsa is, so the combination works really well. And it's such an easy dish to make. You can prepare the fish, place it on a baking tray covered with clingfilm and leave it in the fridge until later that day or evening, so that your main meal will take literally minutes to dish up. You can substitute the cod with haddock or plaice if you prefer. It's also good served with buttered new potatoes.

Serves 4

| 274 | cals | 19.3g | fat | 1.2g | saturates | 6g | sugar | 1.9g | salt |

1 x 400g can chopped tomatoes

1 tablespoon extra virgin olive oil, plus extra for greasing

1 garlic clove, peeled

200g sun-dried tomatoes in oil, drained

1 teaspoon dried chilli flakes

4 fillets of cod, each about 200g, skin on

2 tablespoons freshly chopped chives

Salt

1 Preheat the oven to 190°C/gas mark 5 and lightly oil a baking tray. Put all the ingredients except the cod and the chives in a food processor and blitz to create a smooth creamy paste. Taste to see if it needs a little salt and set aside.

2 Place the cod fillets on the baking tray, skin-side down. Spoon the spicy salsa on top of each fillet, ensuring that the flesh is completely covered. Transfer the tray to the middle of the oven and bake for 16 minutes.

3 Remove the tray from the oven and leave to rest for 1 minute. Sprinkle with the chives and serve with plain boiled rice.

Polli tra brace e mattoni
Marinated poussin cooked under bricks

OK.... Many of you are going to think I've gone nuts with this one but it's a fantastic recipe. Somehow the weight of the brick pressing the meat down over the heat really works and it takes on a subtle smoked flavour. Your guests will be very impressed as likely as not they will never have seen this before (either that or they'll think you're drunk), but you'll definitely be a winner when they taste the end result.

Serves 4

598	cals	44.3g	fat	11g	saturates	0g	sugar	0.0g	salt

4 poussins (baby chicken)

1 teaspoon dried chilli flakes

2 garlic cloves, peeled and crushed

4 tablespoons fresh rosemary leaves

1 tablespoon fennel seeds

30ml olive oil

Salt and freshly ground black pepper

4 bricks

1 Thoroughly scrub the bricks until clean and set aside.

2 Place the poussins on a chopping board. Insert a sharp cooking knife inside the first one and feel for the backbone along the base of the cavity. Press down firmly to cut the first side, then feel for the other side of the backbone and repeat the process. Discard the spine and open out the chicken. Prepare the other three poussins in the same way.

3 Place the flattened poussins on a flat plastic tray and sprinkle over the chilli, garlic, rosemary and fennel seeds. Drizzle with the oil and season with salt and pepper. Massage the marinade all over the poussins, cover with clingfilm and leave in the fridge to marinate for 4 hours.

4 Preheat your griddle pan or barbeque to its hottest setting. Remove the marinated poussins from the fridge 20 minutes before cooking them.

5 Place the poussins on the griddle or barbeque and place a brick on top of each one. Cook for 30 minutes or until cooked through. You can check by inserting a probe – the meat is cooked when the internal temperature reads 85–90°C. Serve with a little cavolo nero.

Rotolo di pollo con spinaci
Rolled chicken breasts stuffed with spinach and rosemary

We cook chicken a lot in our house as most people enjoy it but this doesn't mean it gets boring; you really can be adventurous with the flavours you put with it. This is another meal that takes minutes to prepare yet it looks very special when you serve it. You can do the preparation in the morning and cook when you're ready and although I've suggested this with salad, you can accompany it with almost any vegetable. As a bonus, if there's any left over, try it cold the following day for lunch – it's *fantastico!*

Serves 4

187 cals	2.4g fat	0.6g saturates	2.4g sugar	0.4g salt

4 skinless chicken breasts,
   each about 150g

2 garlic cloves, peeled

1 courgette, chopped

150g frozen spinach, defrosted

1 large round tomato, deseeded

1 tablespoon fresh thyme leaves

Salt and freshly ground
   black pepper

4 sheets of baking parchment

1 Preheat the oven to 200°C/gas mark 6. Place the chicken breasts between two sheets of clingfilm on a chopping board. Using a cooking mallet, bat out each breast to a thickness of about 0.5cm. Discard the clingfilm.

2 Put all the other ingredients except the salad leaves in a food processor and season with salt and pepper. Blitz until everything is finely chopped and combined. Spread the spinach mixture evenly over one side of the chicken breasts. Roll up the breasts to encase the stuffing.

3 Wrap each roll carefully in baking parchment, shaped like a Christmas cracker. Place the parcels on a baking tray and transfer the tray to in the middle of the oven to cook for 30 minutes.

4 Remove the baking tray from the oven and discard the baking parchment. Place the chicken rolls on a chopping board and slice each one into 4 rounds using a sharp knife. Serve immediately, accompanied with a fresh crispy salad.

Coscia di agnello alla brace
Barbecued leg of lamb with rosemary and garlic

If, like me, you love barbecue food but sometimes tire of the traditional chops, steaks or sausages, this is the recipe for you. When lamb is in season, nothing tastes better. The smell alone will make your mouth water. Cooked properly, the meat will be as soft as butter. Do remember to bring the meat to room temperature before cooking (this applies in most cases not just this recipe), because meat cooked straight from the fridge tends to dry on the outside and become tough, while the inside will remain raw.

Serves 6

| 431 cals | 29.2g fat | 8.8g saturates | 1.2g sugar | 0.5g salt |

1.8kg leg of lamb

5 garlic cloves, chopped

3 tablespoons fresh rosemary leaves, chopped

100ml olive oil

100g low-fat thick natural yogurt

Salt and freshly ground black pepper

1 Prepare the leg of lamb by trimming away large areas of solid fat, and then remove the bone by cutting back the meat on either side of it, trying to keep the knife as close as possible to the bone.

2 Open the meat and trim away any excess fat. To butterfly the lamb, slice the thick sides in half and open out. At this point the piece of meat should be twice the size of the original and ready to be marinated. Place the boneless meat into a large, non-metallic serving dish.

3 Combine the remaining ingredients in a large bowl and rub the marinade all over the lamb. Leave the meat to rest in the fridge for 3 hours. Preheat the grill or barbecue.

4 Bring the marinated lamb to room temperature and cook on the hot grill or barbecue for 25 minutes on each side. Use any leftover marinade to baste the meat during cooking.

5 Place the leg of lamb on a chopping board, season with salt and pepper and leave it to rest for 3 minutes to allow the meat to relax and become juicy. Slice and serve with a couscous salad.

Spiedini di polpette
Skewered meatballs with minted yogurt

Meatballs make a hearty meal but you could argue that they can look too rustic for entertaining. This is a perfect way to jazz up your meatballs and make them look more posh. Omitting breadcrumbs lightens the texture, not only making the meatballs healthier but really enhancing the flavour of the lamb and herbs. Instead of tomatoes, you could skewer baby onions or button mushrooms, if you prefer.

Serves 4

286	cals	19.3g	fat	6.2g	saturates	8.7g	sugar	0.5g	salt

300g lean lamb, minced

1 large onion, finely chopped

2 garlic cloves, finely chopped

½ teaspoon dried chilli flakes

2 tablespoons freshly chopped mint

16 cherry tomatoes

4 tablespoons olive oil

Salt to taste

for the dressing

200ml low-fat yogurt

3 tablespoons freshly chopped mint

1 teaspoon dried oregano

Salt and freshly ground black pepper

1 Put the lamb in a large mixing bowl with the onions, garlic, chilli and mint. Season with salt and use your fingertips to mix everything together. Divide the mixture into quarters. Roll out 5 balls from each quarter and set aside.

2 Thread 1 meatball on to a metal skewer, follow by a cherry tomato and continue until you have 5 meatballs and 4 tomatoes on each skewer. Preheat the grill.

3 Transfer the skewers to a baking tray and brush with the oil. Place under the grill for 10 minutes, turning the skewers regularly until browned all over. Meanwhile, pour the yogurt into a bowl and add the mint and oregano. Season with salt and mix together.

4 Place the lamb skewers on a large serving plate and drizzle over the minty yogurt. Serve hot.

Svizzerine

Light lamb burgers with sun-dried tomatoes and pecorino

Fast-food outlets have given burgers a bad reputation but actually they are so simple to make yourself. Biting into a homemade burger is something else. Whenever I have entertained and presented these lamb burgers I've had more of a happy, grateful, excited reaction, than if I'd spent all day in the kitchen, cooking up a difficult dish. This is real comfort food but with so much more flavour than you would expect. If you're *not* being good, top with some bacon and cheese and spread some mayo and English mustard on the bap – yum!

Serves 4

472	cals	26.8g	fat	10.1g	saturates	2.1g	sugar	1.9g	salt

450g lean minced lamb

2 teaspoons finely chopped mint leaves

50g fresh breadcrumbs

4 sun-dried tomatoes in oil, drained and finely chopped

1 garlic clove, peeled and finely chopped

30g Pecorino cheese, freshly grated

1 egg, beaten

Flour for dusting

2 tablespoons olive oil for brushing

2 burger baps, split horizontally

50g mixed salad leaves

Salt and freshly ground black pepper

1 In a large bowl, mix together the minced lamb, mint, breadcrumbs, sun-dried tomatoes, garlic and Pecorino. Season with salt and pepper and stir in the beaten egg to bind the mixture. Lightly flour the palm of your hands and start to shape the meat mixture into 4 equal balls. Gently flatten each ball between your hands to create a burger shape. Preheat a griddle pan.

2 Brush each burger with a little oil and cook on the griddle pan for 4 minutes on each side. Warm the baps in the oven or under a hot grill until crispy.

3 Place a halved bap on 4 serving plates and top with salad leaves. Put a hot burger on each bap. *Buon Appetito!*

Pappardelle con melanzane
Pasta with aubergines, tomatoes and garlic sauce

Many people steer clear of aubergine and yet it really is an easy vegetable to prepare. In this sauce, it enhances the tomato flavour without overpowering it, so if you have children who don't like their vegetables, try this dish – they'll hardly know it's there. I often serve this pasta as a starter but be careful with portion sizes as you don't want to fill everyone up before the main. Tagliatelle can also be used and if you ever have any sauce left, you can use it to accompany a plain grilled fish dish.

Serves 6

| 414 cals | 10.8g fat | 3g saturates | 8.3g sugar | 0.8g salt |

1 vegetable stock cube

3 medium aubergines, about 200g each

1 x 400g can chopped tomatoes

3 garlic cloves, peeled and halved

3 tablespoons extra virgin olive oil

3 tablespoons fresh basil leaves, shredded

3 large plum tomatoes, deseeded and quartered

500g pappardelle

60g freshly grated Parmesan cheese

Salt and freshly ground black pepper

1 Measure 2 litres of water into a large saucepan, drop in the stock cube, and bring to the boil. Prepare the aubergine by trimming away the last 1cm from both ends, along with any green bits. Cut the flesh into 3cm cubes.

2 Cook the cubed aubergine in the boiling stock for 8 minutes. Drain through a colander and set aside to cool. Once the cubes are cooled, slightly squeeze them in the colander so that any excess water drains away.

3 Heat the oil in a large frying pan and gently start to fry the garlic for 1 minute. Add in the aubergine and continue to cook for 5 minutes, stirring occasionally with a wooden spoon. Tip in the chopped tomatoes, season with salt and pepper and continue to cook over a medium heat for 15 minutes, stirring occasionally. Add the basil and the quartered tomatoes and cook for a further 10 minutes, stirring every couple of minutes.

4 Meanwhile, cook the pasta in a large saucepan of salted boiling water until al dente. Once cooked, drain the pasta and tip back into the same pan. Pour over the aubergine sauce and gently stir everything together for 15 seconds to ensure all the flavours combine. Serve immediately sprinkled with a little Parmesan.

Torta di verdure
Fresh vegetable and lemon pie

This is the perfect vegetarian recipe for feeding a crowd. When creating this hearty dish I worried about missing the meat but I found I didn't; in fact it would have ruined it. The pastry gives you another texture and together with the vegetables, it really is a match made in heaven – absolutely *buonissimo!* Of course you can add mushrooms or carrots if you like but I recommend you keep in the leeks and onions for their fuller flavour. *Buon appetito!*

Serves 8

471 cals	31.9g fat	14.1g saturates	10.5g sugar	0.7g salt

6 tablespoons olive oil, plus extra for greasing

2 large red onions, finely sliced

1 tablespoon thyme leaves, finely chopped

2 yellow peppers, cut into 2cm cubes

2 red peppers, cut into 2cm cubes

1 large leek, trimmed, halved lengthways then finely sliced

2 courgettes, trimmed, halved lengthways then sliced 1cm thick

3 eggs

80g grated Parmesan cheese

Zest of 1 large unwaxed lemon

150ml double cream

2 sheets ready-rolled puff pastry

Salt and white pepper

1 Preheat the oven to 180°C/gas mark 4. Use a little oil to grease a 25cm-diameter fluted, loose-based, flan tin. Heat the oil in a large frying pan and start to fry the onions over a medium heat for 3 minutes. Add the thyme with the rest of the vegetables, season with salt and pepper and continue to cook for a further 10 minutes, stirring occasionally. Remove everything from the pan with a slotted spoon and set aside to cool.

2 Whisk together 2 eggs with the Parmesan, lemon zest and the cream, season with salt and pepper.

3 Line the base of the flan tin with one sheet of the puff pastry and arrange the vegetables on top. Pour over the egg mixture and cover with the remaining pastry sheet. Pinch the edges together to secure and trim if necessary.

4 Beat the remaining egg in a bowl and brush over the surface of the pie. Make a little cut in the centre to allow the steam to escape. Transfer to the middle of the oven and bake for 30 minutes until beautiful and golden.

5 Remove the pie from the oven and allow to rest for 5 minutes before pushing it out of the flan tin – it will be easier to cut it into slices. Serve warm, accompanied with a mixed salad.

Budino al cioccolato
Dark chocolate pudding with orange liqueur

I absolutely love puddings and I wanted to create the ultimate chocolate pudding using orange liqueur for a tangy kick. This is a fantastic dessert for entertaining because it not only looks great but you can prepare it before your guests arrive, ready to serve up. It's full of flavour and the Amaretti biscuits give it that extra crunch. You can use any liqueur but I find coffee, orange or brandy work best with chocolate.

Serves 6

307 cals	13.9g fat	5.3g saturates	33.3g sugar	0.2g salt

500ml full-fat milk

15g plain white flour

30g caster sugar

2 teaspoons vanilla extract

80ml orange liqueur

100g dark chocolate
(at least 70% cocoa solids),
finely chopped

30g salted butter

12 Amaretti biscuits (use the
hard ones)

Icing sugar, for dusting

1 Pour the milk in a saucepan and place over a low heat to warm. In a separate medium saucepan, combine the flour, sugar and vanilla extract, pour in a little of the warm milk and mix to create a smooth paste. Pour in the remaining milk and transfer the saucepan to the low heat. Warm up the mixture and whisk continuously to prevent lumps from forming.

2 Stir in the orange liqueur and continue to whisk over a low heat until the mixture begun to thicken – you want it the consistency of thick double cream. Remove the saucepan from the heat and add in the chocolate along with the butter. Keep stirring to ensure all the ingredients are well combined.

3 Divide the chocolate mixture between 6 dessert glasses and leave to set at room temperature for 1 hour. Just before serving my chocolate puddings, crush the Amaretti biscuits over each one and dust with a little icing sugar.

Zuppa Inglese
Amaretti and vanilla trifle

Trifle is one of the best English desserts and there are many variations. I have created a healthier Italian version that is still brimming with the flavours you'd expect but leaves you feeling less heavy and guilty! I serve them individually which always gives the impression of a really special dessert, particularly if you have glass dishes that show off the layers. You can substitute the fruit with blackberries or peaches if you prefer.

Serves 4

310 cals	**10.9g** fat	**2.4g** saturates	**34.5g** sugar	**0.2g** salt

10 amaretti biscuits (use the crunchy version)

4 tablespoons amaretto

120g raspberries

120g blueberries

300ml low-fat custard, ready made

300ml low-fat natural yogurt

1 teaspoon vanilla extract

20g flaked almonds, toasted until lightly brown

2 chocolate flakes, crushed

1 Place the amaretti in a folded tea towel and crush into small pieces. Divide the crushed biscuits between 4 dessert glasses about 8cm in diameter. Pour the amaretto over the biscuits and set aside for 20 minutes.

2 Share out the raspberries and blueberries between the 4 glasses then spoon over enough custard to cover the berries. Mix the yogurt with the vanilla extract and spoon a layer over the custard.

3 Transfer the trifles to the fridge to rest for 45 minutes. Just before serving, scatter over the toasted almonds and sprinkle the chocolate flakes on top. Enjoy!!

Tip

Two small glasses of champagne is 266 calories. Just 30 minutes of cycling will burn off the calories, but a lager or beer is the equivalent of 119 calories. See the back of these calories with 20 minutes of swimming.

Treats

Torta con marmellata senza uova
Egg-free sponge cake with strawberry jam

Whenever I am using eggs during a live food presentation, I always mention that I keep chickens and how amazing it is to have fresh eggs every day. Lucky me – but many people come up to me afterwards to ask if I have any egg-free cake recipes as either they don't like eggs or are allergic to them. So I have come up with an alternative to the traditional Victoria sponge that is made without eggs. You can just as well layer it with raspberry jam or fresh strawberries and whipped cream if you prefer.

Serves 8

278	cals	8.9g	fat	1.1g	saturates	30g	sugar	0.3g	salt

230g self-raising wholemeal flour

2 teaspoons baking powder

170g caster sugar, plus extra for dusting

6 tablespoons sunflower oil, plus extra for oiling

250ml water

2 teaspoons vanilla extract

4 tablespoons strawberry jam

1 Preheat the oven to 190°C/gas mark 5. Oil two 20cm sandwich tins and line the bases with baking parchment. Sift the flour and baking powder into a large mixing bowl and stir in caster sugar. Pour in the oil, water and vanilla extract. Mix with a wooden spoon for about 1 minute until smooth. Divide the mixture between the prepared tins.

2 Transfer to the middle of the oven and bake for 30 minutes. Remove the sponges from the oven and leave to cool in the tins for 20 minutes before turning out onto a wire rack.

3 Once the sponges are completely cool, remove the baking parchment and place one of them on a round serving plate. Spread evenly with the jam and top with the other sponge.

4 Dust the top with a little caster sugar before serving my egg-free sponge cake with a fantastic cup of tea.

Torta di cioccolato e fragole
Chocolate and fresh strawberry cake

Italians from the south don't bake cakes all that often but my sister, Marcella, makes this for me whenever I visit and I love it. The combination of moist chocolate cake and fresh strawberries is wonderful and I can never only have one slice; in fact there is always a fight over who gets the last piece (I normally win!). The cake is also *fantastico* made with raspberries!

Serves 8

| 255 cals | 11.3g fat | 3.7g saturates | 24.6g sugar | 0.8g salt |

150g low fat-spread, plus extra for greasing

130g caster sugar

½ teaspoon ground cinnamon

1½ teaspoons baking powder

2 medium eggs

100g self-raising flour

3 tablespoons cocoa powder

250g fresh strawberries, hulled

130g low-fat thick natural yogurt

1 tablespoon icing sugar

1 chocolate flake, crushed, to decorate

1 Preheat the oven to 190°C/gas mark 5. Lightly grease a 20cm square tin cake and line the base and sides with baking parchment. Put the spread, caster sugar, cinnamon, baking powder and eggs in a large bowl. Sift the flour and cocoa powder into the bowl. Beat with an electric whisk until the mixture is smooth.

2 Pour the cake mixture into the prepared tin and level the surface. Transfer to the middle of the oven and bake for 25 minutes. Remove from the oven and leave the cake to cool slightly in the tin before transferring to a wire rack to cool completely.

3 Halve the strawberries then reserve about a quarter of them on a plate. Place the rest in a medium bowl. Add the yogurt and the icing sugar and gently fold everything together.

4 Spoon the strawberry mixture over the chocolate sponge and decorate the top with the reserved strawberry halves. Sprinkle over the chocolate flake and serve with your favourite hot drink.

Torta leggera al limone
Super-light lemon sponge

There is nothing better than having a cup of tea in the afternoon with a piece of homemade cake and I find a light lemon cake leaves me feeling satisfied, because I've had a treat and feel pampered but I don't feel too full before dinner. I have created many variations of lemon cakes but this one gives you an option of a delicious cake that is incredibly low in fat and calories without compromising on taste.

Serves 16

202 cals	11.3g fat	2g saturates	10.8g sugar	0.2g salt

1 tablespoon butter, for greasing

Juice and zest of 1 large unwaxed lemon

150g caster sugar

160ml low-fat natural yogurt

150ml sunflower oil

270g self-raising flour

2 large eggs

1 Preheat the oven to 160°C/gas mark 3. Grease a 20cm diameter round cake tin with butter and line the base with baking parchment. Pour the lemon juice into a small bowl and mix in 1 tablespoon of sugar. Set aside.

2 Place the lemon zest in a large bowl and add the remaining sugar with the yogurt, oil, flour and eggs. Use a wooden spoon to mix everything together for 1 minute. Pour the mixture into the prepared cake tin and transfer to the middle of the oven to bake for 55 minutes or until risen and springy when touched.

3 Remove the cake from the oven and stand the tin on a cooling rack. Slowly spoon the lemon juice over the hot cake. Allow it to cool down completely in the tin before turning out.

4 Once completely cooled, slice my lemon sponge into 16 portions and enjoy with your afternoon tea.

Torta al cioccolato senza farina
Wheat-free chocolate cake with walnuts

So many people suffer from allergies and I always want my books to include something for everyone. This one is for those who can't eat wheat, although you will never know that it isn't a 'normal' cake so all your guests will enjoy it. It's perfect served warm for afternoon tea, and just as good the following morning with your coffee or tea. If you do save some cake for the next day make sure it's stored in a sealed container to keep the moisture in.

Serves 20

294 cals	23.4g fat	11.1g saturates	14g sugar	0.1g salt

400g good-quality dark chocolate (at least 70% cocoa solids)

180g unsalted butter, plus extra for greasing

6 large eggs, separated

150g caster sugar

4 teaspoons vanilla extract

150g walnut halves, roughly chopped

Pinch of salt

1 Preheat the oven to 180°C/gas mark 4. Grease a 22cm diameter springform cake tin with butter and line the base and sides with baking parchment. Place the chocolate and butter in a small saucepan over a low heat. Stir until melted then set aside to cool, stirring frequently.

2 Whisk the egg yolks with half the sugar in a large mixing bowl until pale and fluffy. Slowly fold the warm chocolate mixture into the egg yolks, and then fold in the vanilla extract, along with the walnuts.

3 Whisk the egg whites with the salt in a large, clean mixing bowl until soft peaks form. Gradually add in the remaining sugar and continue to whisk until firm peaks form. Use a large metal spoon to gently fold the egg whites into the chocolate mixture, a little at a time.

4 Pour the mixture into the prepared cake tin and transfer to the middle of the oven to bake for 50 minutes. The cake is cooked once the top is puffed and slightly cracked. A dry spaghetti strand inserted into the centre should come out with moist crumbs attached.

Crespelle al cioccolato
Chocolate and vanilla pancakes

This is a weekend must in our house: we always have chocolate pancakes on Sunday morning. This recipe is so delicious and easy and is the basis of my family's orders. My eldest son, Luciano, likes it just as is; Rocco, my youngest son, always adds bananas, and I always add crushed hazelnuts. I guarantee these really do begin a perfect Sunday, and they're a wonderful way to round off any meal. If you find you have no chocolate in the cupboard, use a couple of tablespoons of chocolate spread – very naughty but very nice!

Serves 4

309 cals	15g fat	7.6g saturates	12.9g sugar	0.3g salt

100g plain white flour
2 teaspoons cocoa powder
Pinch of salt
1 large egg
300ml skimmed milk
2 teaspoons olive oil

for the sauce

160ml skimmed milk
1 teaspoon vanilla extract
120g good-quality dark chocolate (at least 70% cocoa solids), chopped into small pieces

1 Sift the flour, cocoa powder and salt into a large mixing bowl. Add the egg and milk and whisk together until smooth. Heat a small, heavy-based frying pan. Add a few drops of oil and pour in some batter. Tilt the pan so that the mixture spread evenly over the base to make a thin pancake.

2 As soon as the pancake has set on the surface, flip it over to cook the other side. Make 8 pancakes in total, transferring them to a sheet of kitchen paper as you cook them. When all pancakes are cooked, fold them into triangles.

3 Wipe the frying pan with a sheet of kitchen paper, and then pour in the milk. Add the vanilla and the chocolate pieces to the milk. Heat gently to melt the chocolate.

4 Return all the pancakes to the frying pan, overlapping them to fit. Cook gently for 30 seconds. Serve 2 pancakes per person and pour over any remaining chocolate sauce from the pan.

Crespelle con limone e Grand Marnier

Pancakes with lemon and Grand Marnier

OK, it's raining outside, you had a light lunch and it's around 3pm... who fancies a special pancake treat? Here it is – the recipe takes only a few minutes to rustle up and is worth every bit of your time. My pancakes are packed with flavour yet not heavy at all. They're perfect for dessert after a heavy meal, too. Whoever you make this for will definitely feel special, so be sure to make it for yourself sometimes.

Serves 4

204 cals	3.9g fat	0.9g saturates	12g sugar	0.3g salt

100g plain white flour

Pinch of salt

1 large egg

300ml skimmed milk

Zest and juice of 1 unwaxed lemon

2 teaspoons olive oil

1 tablespoon caster sugar

3 tablespoons Grand Marnier liqueur

1 Sift the flour and salt into a large mixing bowl. Add the egg, milk and lemon zest and whisk together until smooth. Heat a small, heavy-based frying pan. Add a few drops of oil and spoon in 2 tablespoons of the batter. Tilt the pan so that the mixture spread evenly over the base to make a thin pancake.

2 As soon as the pancake has set on the surface, flip it over to cook the other side. Make 8 pancakes in total, transferring them to a sheet of kitchen paper as you cook them. When all pancakes are cooked, fold them into triangles.

3 Wipe the frying pan clean with a sheet of kitchen paper, and then pour in the lemon juice and the sugar. Heat gently to dissolve the sugar then pour in the Grand Marnier.

4 Return all the pancakes to the frying pan, overlapping them to fit. Cook gently for 30 seconds. Serve 2 pancakes per person and enjoy with a glass of freshly squeezed orange juice.

Cioccolatini con noccioline
Mini chocolate and nut bites

How cool would it be to create your own chocolate bar, to know exactly what's in it and enjoy your homemade treat whenever you fancy? This is my little gift for all you chocoholics out there! You can be as creative as you like with your bars, using different nuts or dried fruits, even honeycomb or crushed biscuits. The only problem you will cause by making my *cioccolatini* is sharing them!

Makes about 65 pieces

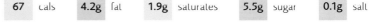

67 cals	4.2g fat	1.9g saturates	5.5g sugar	0.1g salt

350g good-quality dark chocolate, 70% cocoa solids, roughly chopped

1 x 400g can condensed skimmed milk

40g salted butter

Pinch of Maldon sea salt

100g pistachios, skinned

50g hazelnuts

Icing sugar, to decorate

1 Put the chocolate, condensed milk, butter and salt in a heavy-based saucepan over a low heat. Stir everything together using a wooden spoon until melted. Put the nuts in a freezer bag and bash them with a rolling pin until broken into pieces. Stir the nuts into the chocolate mixture.

2 Pour the mixture into a foil tray measuring about 22cm square and smooth the top using a flexible spatula. Put the tray in the fridge for 5 hours until set.

3 Transfer the chocolate slab from the tray to a chopping board. Cut into 3cm square pieces. Pile the *cioccolatini* in the middle of a serving plate and dust with a little icing sugar before serving them with a cup of tea.

4 If you have any *cioccolatini* left over, put them in a plastic container and freeze.

Tazzine di cioccolato
Chocolate and hazelnut cups

This is quite a rich mousse and the nuts make it more filling so the amount is just perfect and looks very cute served in espresso cups. If you prefer, use pistachios instead of hazelnuts.

Serves 4

307	cals	17.5g	fat	5.2g	saturates	28.4g	sugar	0.1g	salt

2 large eggs, separated

60g caster sugar

85g good-quality dark chocolate (at least 70% cocoa solids), broken into pieces, plus 15g piece, grated, to decorate

150ml 0% fat Greek-style yogurt

50g crushed hazelnuts

1 Whisk the egg yolks with the sugar in a large mixing bowl until pale and fluffy. Put the chocolate pieces in a medium heatproof bowl and place over a saucepan of simmering water until melted. Remove from the heat and set aside to cool slightly.

2 Whisk the melted chocolate into the egg yolks. Fold the yogurt into the chocolate mixture until smooth.

3 Whisk the egg whites in a large, clean mixing bowl until stiff peaks form then use a large metal spoon to gently fold them into the chocolate mixture with the hazelnuts.

4 Spoon the mixture into 4 espresso cups and refrigerate for 1 hour. Just before serving, sprinkle with the grated chocolate.

Fragole con meringhe e panna
Strawberry and Amaretto Eton Mess

Serves 4

251	cals	15.2g	fat	9.5g	saturates	26.2g	sugar	0.1g	salt

500g strawberries, hulled

1 teaspoon caster sugar

1 tablespoon Amaretto liqueur

150ml whipping cream

4 small meringue nests, ready made

1 Quarter the strawberries and place in a medium bowl. Add the sugar and Amaretto and gently mix everything together. Leave to macerate for 5 minutes.

2 Pour the cream in a large bowl and whip until thick but still soft. Roughly crumble the meringue nests into the cream.

3 Set aside 100g of the macerated strawberries and fold the rest into the cream and crushed meringues. Spoon the mess into 4 serving glasses and top each one with some of the reserved strawberries. Serve immediately and enjoy!

Fragole e caramello
Strawberries in Cointreau with crunchy topping

For those of you who want to serve up dessert but still want to be very careful with your calorie/fat intake, this one is definitely for you. It looks lovely and the caramel topping gives it a special touch, but at the end of the day it's strawberries and low-fat yogurt poshed up. No one will even know they are being healthy as the liqueur and caramel give it that sweet special flavour. Enjoy.

Serves 4

221	cals	1g	fat	0.6g	saturates	42g	sugar	0.2g	salt

350g strawberries, hulled and quartered

Juice of ½ orange

4 tablespoons Cointreau liqueur

350g low-fat natural yogurt

for the topping

100g caster sugar

2 tablespoons cold water

1 Divide the strawberries between 4 glasses about 6cm high. Drizzle over the orange juice and the Cointreau. Spoon the yogurt on top and chill until ready to serve.

2 To prepare the topping, tip the sugar into a small saucepan with the water. Heat gently, stirring with a tablespoon until the sugar dissolves. Increase the heat and stop stirring. Carefully boil the sugar mixture until it turns a light caramel colour. Quickly remove from the heat and plunge the base of the pan into a sink filled with cold water to stop it cooking any further.

3 When the bubbles have subsided, carefully pour the caramel over each dessert. Leave to rest at room temperature for 10 minutes before serving.

Tip

If you just couldn't help yourself from devouring a Snickers bar (271 calories)...
... then you'll need to go for a 50 minute walk in order to burn it off!

If you ate a Kit Kat (218 calories)...
... you'll need to put on your trainers and go for a 30 minute run!

The Five-Minute Metabolism Boosting Workout

Think you don't have time to exercise your way to a fabulous body? Think again! This all new five-minute Italian body plan couldn't be easier. Who wouldn't like to have the honed, toned and super-fit figure of one of Italy's finest beach babes? The good news is that getting that enviable body is considerable more achievable (and affordable!) than you might think, with no expensive gyms, gruelling personal training sessions or punishing 5am cardio workouts.

Celebrity trainer Nicki Waterman has designed an ultra-easy fitness plan that's designed to fit around even the most frantic schedule. Her metabolism-boosting regime consists of a range of five-minute mini-workouts that draw on compound exercises (where you target more than one muscle group at once), plyometric or jump-based training, interval workouts, Pilates and yoga. Stick to *La Dolce Diet* recipes and this exercise plan, you should expect to lose a steady 1½ lb per week.

The fitness plan is ultra-flexible. You choose one or more workout segments to do in the morning, afternoon or at night – whenever you have time. When you're busy, do less and on days when you have an hour to yourself, do a lot more! As a guide, aim for an average of two complete mini-workouts a day: ideally a combination of the metabolism boosting routine and the five-minute cardio blast walking/jogging workout. By squeezing in all the workout segments throughout your day, you can shape up super-fast, without having to find a big block of workout time in your day.

NOTE: Please check with your doctor before starting any exercise programme.

The Exercise Plan

Pick two sessions a day from Blast A, Blast B and the cardio workout. Simply intersperse the outdoor cardio (a short walk or jog) with the blast circuits at home. You'll need two weights or 500ml bottles of water.

Cardio Blast Workout

For the walking or jogging cardio blast, 10 is maximum effort (you shouldn't be able to sustain this pace for more than 30 seconds!) while 0 would be totally sedentary. Start at an effort level you feel comfortable with and build-up gradually. If you're not up to jogging, don't worry – just stick to a fast walking pace.

WALKING OR JOGGING

2 minute	Warm-up walk	at 3.5
1 minute	Slow jog	5mph
30 seconds	Fast jog	6mph
1 minute	Jog	5mph
30 seconds	Fast jog	6.5mph
30 seconds	Jog	5mph
30 seconds	Cool down walk	3.5mph

How to burn 500 calories a day without really trying

Did you know that doing everyday jobs like washing the dishes by hand and taking the stairs instead of the lift helps you burn an extra 111 calories per day than if you let modern conveniences do all the work?

And using up that many extra calories every day could help you lose 12lbs in a year. If you incorporate the metabolism boosting exercises too, the calorie burn will be profound...

7.30 AM

Make your bed instead of leaving it all rumpled – in fact, why not put on fresh sheets while you're at it?

You'll burn: 40 calories

8.45 AM

Park in the spot that's farthest from your office or train and power-walk there (about three minutes each way).

You'll burn: 50 calories

10.20 AM

Forget email! Walk to colleagues' desks and deliver the messages in person instead.

You'll burn: 75 calories

12:35 PM

Take the stairs rather than the lift when you go to grab lunch, plus when you get to work and leave (six flights each way).

You'll burn: 90 calories

3.15 PM

Offer to do the afternoon coffee run – but instead of going to the kitchen, take a walk to a coffee shop.

You'll burn: 75 calories

5.45 PM

Leave the supermarket trolley in the store and carry the shopping bags to the car yourself – and into the house too.

You'll burn: 45 calories

7.20 PM

Give your dishwasher the night off and wash a load of dishes by hand instead (for half an hour).

You'll burn: 55 calories

8.30 PM

Get off the sofa and pace around the room while you chat on the phone with a friend for 20 minutes.

You'll burn: 70 calories

Blast A

BOUNCING BALL SHUFFLE

1 Stand with your feet shoulder-width apart, knees slightly bent, hands in front of your torso as if holding a ball.

2 Shuffle four steps to one side, moving your arms up and down as if bouncing a ball.

3 Repeat on the opposite side and continue, alternating sides, for one minute.

SPLIT LUNGE AND WALK

1 Stand in an exaggerated power walk stance with knees and arms bent.

2 Jump in the air, switching your arms and legs as you jump, so you land with your other leg and arm in front. Continue for one minute.

PLANK AND ROW

1 Holding two weights or 500ml bottles of water shoulder-width apart on the floor, get into a bend-knee push-up position. Contract your abs, so that there's a straight line from your shoulders to your knees.

2 Bend your right elbow and draw your right shoulder blade towards the middle of your back. Lower your hand to the floor, keeping your abs contracted for support.

Do one set of 10 repetitions on each side.

SIDE LUNGE AND ROW

1 Take two weights (500ml bottles of water are great for this). Stand with your legs together, knees slightly bent, and your arms by sides.

2 Inhale and take a wide step to the side with your toes facing forwards. Bend your knee and reach your arms towards the bent knee.

3 Exhale and push off your bent leg, bringing your legs together. At the same time bring your shoulder blades together with your elbows behind your body. Your upper body should be pitched slightly forwards.

Do one set of 10 repetitions on each side.

CHOPPING WOOD

1 Take two weights or 500ml bottles of water. Stand with your feet shoulder-width apart with your feet turned out and knees bent. Bend your arms and rest both weights on your right hip.

2 Exhale and straighten both knees as you rotate your torso towards the left. At the same time move your arms across your body towards your left shoulder. Inhale and bend your knees, returning your hands to your right hip.

Do one set of 10 repetitions on each side.

Blast B

DOUBLE PULSE SQUATS AND JUMP

1 Stand with your feet shoulder-width apart, knees slightly bent and arms at your sides. Bend your knees, keeping your weight in your heels. Pulse up and down twice.

2 Spring off the floor and jump up and forwards, reaching both arms up. Land back in a squat position, pulse up and down twice and jump up and back to your starting position.

   Repeat for one minute.

HAMSTRING CURLS WITH TRICEP EXTENSION

1 Take two weights or 500ml bottles of water. Stand on your right leg with your left leg bent and lifted about 60cm off the floor behind you. Lean forwards from your hips and place your left hand on your left hip. Extend your right arm behind your body with palm facing in.

2 Inhale and bring your left leg in front of you with the knee bent to waist height and your right arm to your side. Exhale and extend your arm and leg back to the start position.

   Do one set of 10 repetitions on each leg.

FLAMINGO WITH BICEP CURL

1 Take two weights or 500ml bottles of water. Stand with your weight on your right leg with your left leg extended behind you and resting on your toe.

2 Inhale as you bend your right leg and lift your left leg off the floor. At the same time, lift your right arm to shoulder height. Exhale and return to the start position.

Do one set of 10 repetitions on each side.

PRETEND SKIPPING

1 Stand with your feet shoulder-width apart and your arms bent as if holding a skipping rope.

2 Spring from one foot to the other while moving your arms as if you were turning a skipping rope.

Continue for one minute.

SQUAT LIFT WITH LATERAL SIDE LIFTS

1 Take two weights or 500ml bottles of water. Stand with your feet shoulder-width apart in a squat position. Holding the weights at your side, bend your arms slightly.

2 Extend both knees and contract your abs. Lift your right leg off the floor to the side of your body and extend your arms to shoulder height.

Do one set of 10 repetitions on each side.

Index